INNER PEACE
OUTER POWER

T0059309

INNER PEACE

OUTER POWER

A Shamanic Guide to
LIVING YOUR PURPOSE

SHAMAN
NABEEL REDWOOD

Hierophantpublishing

Copyright © 2022 by Nabeel Redwood

All rights reserved, including the right to reproduce this work
in any form whatsoever, without permission in writing from the
publisher, except for brief passages in connection with a review.

Cover design by Emma Smith
Cover art by Jr Korpa | Unsplash
abrakadabra | Shutterstock
Nadezhda Shuparskaia | Shutterstock
Teo Tarras | Shutterstock
Print book interior design by Frame25 Productions

Hierophant Publishing
San Antonio, TX
www.hierophantpublishing.com

If you are unable to order this book from your local bookseller,
you may order directly from the publisher.

Library of Congress Control Number: 2022930405
ISBN 978-1-950253-21-0
10 9 8 7 6 5 4 3 2 1

≈

Note: The names and identifying details of people associated
with events described in this book have been changed.
Any similarity to actual persons is coincidental.

For Katelyn, the greatest warrior I know.

When you are in doubt, be still, and wait; when doubt no longer exists for you, then go forward with courage. So long as mists envelop you, be still; be still until the sunlight pours through and dispels the mists—as it surely will. Then act with courage.

—Chief White Eagle

Contents

Introduction

*Every human is an artist. The dream
of your life is to make beautiful art.*
—don Miguel Ruiz, *The Four Agreements*

From the ancient Vedic traditions of India, or the Sufi school in Islam, or the native tribes of what are now called the Americas, spiritual traditions around the world have often described life as a dream.

This means that right now, as you read this, you are dreaming.

The strangest, and potentially frustrating, part is that we all arrived here in this great dream world with almost no recollection of how we got here and no instructions for what we are supposed to do or how to go about doing it . . . and in fact, most of us *don't even know we are dreaming*. We work and play and argue and sing and carry on as if this is all there is: rocked by the onslaught of life's ups and downs, we play the game and perform our parts without pausing to wonder why.

Then, inevitably, there comes a time in our life when the dream we're living doesn't go as we'd planned. Perhaps something tragic occurs, or we fail to reach a goal we aspired to. When life hands us our share of the inevitable disappointments we all face and things don't work out as we had planned, what do we do then?

That's what happened to me.

See, when I was a kid, I knew I wanted to be an artist. As I grew up, I convinced myself I was meant to be an artist. And by the time I was an adult, I believed I was *destined* to be an artist. But just when it looked as if I was on the cusp of attaining everything I desired, my life utterly fell apart. My prospects for a career in art evaporated, and I was stuck in a job I hated, barely making ends meet. What's worse is that in my desperate pursuit of "artistic success," I had neglected family, alienated friends, and ignored every other area of my life. My dream had become a nightmare. After years of chasing my dreams and falling short, I was lost. I'd been so certain of my path that I even felt the universe itself had betrayed me.

In a desperate quest to pull myself out of the dark hole I was in, I ravenously studied every spiritual tradition, teaching, and technique I could find in hopes of uncovering an answer.

Eventually, I found that answer in shamanism.

Shamanism is a collection of earth-based teachings and mystic techniques found in many of the indigenous cultures of the world. Largely drawing its wisdom from nature, shamanism is largely concerned with living a life of peace and *power*: how we can develop it, how we can use it, and how we often lose it.

Shamanism also teaches that the reality we perceive in our daily lives is a dream. Our failure to realize it as such can create problems, but when we finally do wake up to this fact, we find that we have an incredible opportunity to create our own reality as we see fit—and shamanism provides the tools to do exactly that. Once I understood this, I realized that I had been dreaming all wrong. With practice, I came to see my life as a little dream alongside everyone else's little dream and that we dream up the Big Dream of reality together.

Through the guidance and training of some wonderful healers and teachers, I learned to regain the power I had lost and even became a healer and teacher myself in the process. Not only did I learn to dream again, but I began to dream with power. My teachers showed me that we're each here to live the dream of our choosing.

The ideas I found in shamanism were very different than most traditional religious paths. What our culture tends to refer to as "traditional" spirituality is often centered on either theism (bowing to a god until they save you) or renunciation (meditating in a cave until you transcend all human concerns). Shamanism offers a different approach, one where it's possible to thrive in the world, enjoy relationships with others, and make a difference in human affairs, not bow down or run away to escape it all.

I call this alternative to theism and renunciation *the path of the happy warrior*. While this phrase was coined by William Wordsworth in his poem "Character of the Happy Warrior," many shamanic and mystic traditions around the world feature happy warrior characters to learn from and emulate. For example, laughing Buddha images found throughout China come from tales of an eccentric monk whose unconventional wisdom taught valuable lessons about the nature of Zen. Trickster myths from American Indian traditions also often embody the happy warrior in their adventures. There are even modern-day examples in contemporary pop culture, such as the wandering doctor in the British TV show *Doctor Who*, who meets all changes (including shapeshifting genders) and challenges with enthusiasm and curiosity.

Put simply, a happy warrior is someone who perseveres through hardship while keeping a positive outlook. They live confidently with a playful spirit, always doing their best but never taking themselves too seriously. Even when life gets hard, they're happy to be alive. Empowered by joy, they lift up everyone around them.

While my path is shamanic in origin, the teachings and techniques in this book are in fact universal and can be found in an enormous array of traditions. And while there may be times on this journey when we need to retreat to a mountaintop for space and reflection, our goal is always the attainment of inner peace and its natural expression of outer power, bringing both back into the world with us when we return. Those who walk this path don't reject or escape reality but embrace it fully. We develop our own power and use it for healing ourselves, others, and nature. We roll up our sleeves and get involved with reality.

The happy warrior derives their power from an inner foundation of peace and then exercises that power in the outside world in a purposeful way. They align and balance their varying powers for maximum efficacy. They use action and rest as complementary strategies to cultivate and capture their dreams and desires. Equipped to handle the ups and downs, the happy warrior ultimately lives a life that's bursting with meaning even amid hardship. As happy warriors, we can more peacefully enjoy what is already present, create and cultivate what we imagine might be, and overcome obstacles and adversity without losing our good nature. We strive to wake up in the dream of our life and more intentionally cocreate our future. As you can imagine, this is easier said than done, but it is exactly what you will learn to do in this book.

This book is based on my experience as a shamanic healer and spiritual teacher over the past decade and informed by the hundreds of clients I have helped as the founder of Shamanic Healing LA. The teachings and techniques I offer in this book are the same ones I teach to my clients, and they're aimed to cultivate an inner foundation of peace that results in the manifestation of outer power. There is an inherent connection between inner peace and outer power, and we will cover that relationship in detail in the pages that follow. But before we go further, I need to explain what I mean by *power*.

Power can be a tricky word—for many, especially in the context of history, this word has meant power *over* something or someone. This is the kind of power that comes at the expense of another, that dictates that for every winner there must be a loser, and that there is a limited amount of real power to be seized and lorded over others. This dynamic plays out in ways large and small, from the devastating effects of war and violence to intraoffice politics and toxic relationships. This is decidedly *not* the definition of power we are talking about in this book.

When I say *power* here, I am referring to personal power over oneself. You can possess as much of this power as you need without taking any away from anyone else. Personal power is strength, patience, and fortitude. It is the energy source from which we draw the ability to meet every event in our lives, whether positive or negative, with grace and equanimity. It gives us the wherewithal to pursue self-understanding and then act decisively out of that understanding of our authentic needs and goals. When we are in possession of true personal power, we have no desire to dominate others—we become agents of cooperation, healing, and growth instead of competition, corruption, and destruction. When we are dispossessed of our personal power, all aspects of our lives are weakened, and it's easy for emotions like despair and helplessness to color our days and nights.

So how do we lose our personal power?

Power loss is ultimately rooted in how we respond to the universal challenges everyone faces as we journey through life: heartache, loss, trauma, rejection, illness. Denial of our own part in creating these situations can lead to the loss of personal power, as can blame or apathy. We may also respond by turning to temporary remedies that make us feel better in the moment but don't address the root source of the problem—and if left unchecked, these aids might become our addictions. Sadly, I've seen this happen time and again.

As we lose personal power, we become less able to draw on that power to meet new challenges, which further weaken us, leading us toward an increasing sense of emptiness. As we succumb to that emptiness, we lose even more power. It's a dangerous spiral to get caught in. We all have dreams and desires we wish to fulfill, but without power we can't create them. When we lose our personal power, we feel *overpowered by the world* instead.

For example, you may wish to find love and partnership, start a family, become an entrepreneur, or devote yourself to charitable endeavors and create a better world.

These are all worthy goals. But if you don't do the work to establish an inner foundation of peace that manifests outer power, you will likely find that your dreams will be stymied by external forces. Whether these forces are minor setbacks or major roadblocks doesn't matter, as they are actually a reflection of what's happening inside you.

Life will always present challenges on the warrior's path—no worthy goal is easily achieved—but it is how you meet these challenges that dictates whether you will attain your heart's desires.

Until we do the necessary work, our inner critic may step in and subdue us, or we may become paralyzed by fear of failure or squander opportunities because we don't act. Or just as damaging, perhaps our ego goes to the other extreme, and we don't take challenges seriously enough, assuming that everything will come easy for us only to later become frustrated, embittered, and angry when things don't go our way.

During such times of doubt, defeat, lack of direction, or overconfidence, the thing we lose is our power.

This cycle can be stopped, however. Power loss is neither inevitable nor irreversible. The key to regaining and maintaining your store of personal outer power is the cultivation of inner peace.

Inner Peace Leads to Outer Power

Personal power comes from inner peace. Like with the term *power*, there may be some confusion about what I mean by *peace*. In this context, I don't mean peace as in general satisfaction with a situation or condition; I mean being emotionally and mentally relaxed regardless of the situation or condition. It's only from this place of true clarity that we can accurately assess whatever challenge is before us.

What I have found is that personal power comes from a state of peace that doesn't depend on any condition or circumstance. It is consistently there, undergirding every moment and every breath. If you want to regain your personal power, you must cultivate a ground of inner peace.

Well sure, you might be thinking, *but it's not like achieving inner peace is a snap.*

It's true that this kind of unconditional contentment isn't something we're able to reach overnight; but inner peace is not as elusive as you might think. You actually experience it multiple times a day—for example, while drifting off to sleep, basking in a hot shower, or getting lost in a sunset.

By consciously working to surrender to these everyday moments of inner peace, you will eventually discover that it becomes your natural state again. With practice, you'll find inner peace in your own breath and physical sensations, and eventually, you can maintain a state of contentment that doesn't depend on anything outside yourself.

Being at peace means you're calm but aware, fully present in the moment without resistance. Presence and peace occur simultaneously; one cannot exist without the other. When present, you naturally have the power to know, say, and do whatever needs to be known, said, or done in that moment. By doing what the moment calls for, you feed your personal power in each moment.

Yes, the world is full of people who appear to be powerful and exert force over others, but this type of power never lasts. Even when someone attains their desired objectives this way, it will be empty and short-lived. So, while one can misuse and abuse personal powers to claw their desires from reality, it never results in inner peace. True power comes from inner peace, not the other way around, and it is never about mastery over *others*, but *self*-mastery. So it's crucial to find peace in your own body, heart, mind, and spirit to maximize your power effectively.

When you live your life from a state of mind that makes inner peace your top priority, then you're a happy warrior. Prioritizing a foundation of inner peace does not mean you won't have challenges as you pursue your dreams and desires, but rather you can pursue your dreams while effectively dealing with any setbacks or unforeseen changes life sends your way.

From a place of peace, your playful spirit will remain undeterred amid hardship because you won't take yourself or life too seriously. Your joy will drive you to form intimate bonds and deep relationships. Your compassion will compel you to participate as a force for good in the world, using your power in ways large and small to help the powerless. And when needed, you'll stand ready to fight for the greater good, but always with humility, honor, and honesty.

So really, only one question remains: How? How do we live as a happy warrior? How can we create and capture our dreams? My hope is that the following chapters will give you all the tools you need to begin your journey.

We'll start with using mindfulness and meditation techniques to find peace and power in the body. Our physical experience is a crucial part of our life here on earth, so we're going to slow down and see what our senses are telling us.

From there, we'll move on to finding peace and power in the heart. So many of us are guided by emotion, or maybe we've been conditioned to suppress our feelings because they've proved unreliable and problematic in the past. In any case, we're going to practice honoring the heart and opening to new ways of being vulnerable and open.

Next, we'll look at fostering peace and power in the mind, our center for logic and reason—and perhaps the most dominant aspect of our selves. We'll talk about why you can't think your way into finding your life's purpose and learn some techniques for opening up the mind to new perspectives and worldviews.

Finally, we'll dive in to peace and power in the spirit. Ah, the mystical section. This is where my extensive training with leaders in shamanism, reiki, yoga, meditation, indigenous magic, and tarot will benefit our path. We'll use practices to help us grow spiritually, and we'll challenge ourselves to indulge our creative and curious spirit.

Once we are balanced in body, heart, mind, and spirit, we're ready to talk about how we approach life, how we want our path to look moving forward. I'm inspired by two ways of being, which may seem to be in opposition to one another but are actually complementary: the Way of the Gardener and the Way of the Hunter. Yes, we're focused ultimately on being a happy warrior, and I think that metaphor encompasses it all. But we have a lot to learn from the patient planning and tending of the humble gardener and the confident grace and strength of the hunter. We'll incorporate some of the best traits of these two to retrofit our practice.

And in the end we'll put it all together to chart a path and prepare you for the twists, turns, bumps, and about-faces that will surely happen. You'll be equipped with ancient techniques that have proven to offer balance and resilience, and you will be able to navigate your way with confidence. You'll also have a better sense of when to align with a creative impulse and when to let it lie—a crucial skill when life is too short and we're all pressed for time.

I hope this book is a helpful guide to you as you explore what you want and need out of life, and as you sort through your past to imagine a brighter future. We all have work to do, and with the right tools this work can be a joy. And remember, as the saying goes, it's about the journey—not the destination. Let's begin.

Chapter One

The Gift of Presence

When we think of inner peace, we might imagine monks meditating on remote mountaintops and assume that one must achieve this type of spiritual mastery in order to experience peace. But inner peace is actually much less mysterious or supernatural than we typically make it out to be. In fact, you experience inner peace all the time . . . in small, fleeting doses. The truth is that inner peace is actually your default state of being.

Here's what I mean: You've probably experienced moments in your life when your mind—shocked by an intensely dangerous or joyful experience—simply stopped. In that moment between thoughts, you perceived a spacious sense of clarity, as though you were witnessing pure reality before your mind had a chance to say anything about it. It might have happened when you unexpectedly saw a loved one after a long time, or during a car accident. It could have been seemingly mundane and organic: a gust of wind carrying the scent of smoke, sunlight hitting water in a particularly beautiful way. All kinds of experiences can shock the mind into silence and bring you completely into the present moment.

Inner peace is a nonverbal state that only exists in the present. When you bask in a hot shower and the first blast of burning water empties your mind for a moment of bliss, that's inner peace. When you become so totally absorbed in your work, play, or physical activity that you're not thinking of the past or future, that's inner peace. When you lose yourself contemplating the mystery of the sun or stars, that's inner peace. When you're totally captivated in a deep conversation, that's inner peace. In fact, when you first wake up in the morning, you begin the day in this state of inner peace. And you return to this state at night, right before you fall asleep.

It should be evident then that the peace I'm describing here is not a state of feeling good or being satisfied with your circumstances. In all the examples above, your mind momentarily stops, and your awareness becomes totally absorbed in the present moment. It's not dependent on you thinking/feeling the present moment is "good" or "bad." It only depends on you not thinking at all.

Peace is therefore your default way of being, but the busy mind has a habit of overlaying stories onto your reality, many of which can trigger you and knock you out of your peaceful default. Examples of mental stories are, "I am smart/stupid," "they are beautiful/ugly," "this situation is good/bad." As true as these sentences may feel, they're only subjective descriptions that may not have any relation to reality. We may (and often do) indulge in negative stories that make us feel powerless—*I can't do it, it won't work, that's impossible*—and then eventually depressed and defeated. But indulging in positive stories that initially feel empowering—*I can do anything, victory is guaranteed, all my dreams will come true*—can lead to feeling dejected and disheartened when reality turns the other way. No matter how things are going for us at this moment, we can be sure that at some point in the future things will change—because we live in a world of constantly shifting polarities.

In either case, the stories themselves—regardless of whether they're positive or negative—are a distraction, an unnecessary waste of power that sets you up for disappointment. When you disengage from all the mental stories that you tell yourself about yourself, others, and the world, then you stop directing attention and energy toward those stories. That frees up power for you to use more intentionally.

You might object here and say that without your mental storytelling, how could you make sense of the world? How could you participate in society and accomplish your goals?

First, it's important to point out that I'm not talking about ignoring logic and reason. The mind is one of our four major powers and can be very helpful when it comes to determining who you are and what you want to do with your life, but only if you are aware of its inherent storytelling capacity and are able to see the stories as they appear and refuse to become attached to them. Inner peace allows you to do just that: to become aware of the storytelling mind and then choose to not let it control you.

There's a part of you that knows what I'm saying here is true. Consider all the worrying you've done in your life. Did those mental stories ever affect the outcome? Probably not. How many of your worst fears came true? Probably very few. In fact, I'd bet the worst events of your life were totally unexpected tragedies you never worried about happening to you. As for the fearful worries that did come true, would they have happened if you weren't worrying about them? If yes, then your worrying made no difference. If not, then maybe worrying was a self-fulfilling prophecy. So why take the chance with worrying when at best it makes no difference and at worst it actively manifests the feared outcome?

It's far more likely that every great idea you've had, every profound realization you've received, every confident decision you've ever made occurred spontaneously. These great ideas, profound realizations, and confident decisions probably came to you when you were absorbed in the moment. Maybe you were having a great conversation that prompted an epiphany. Maybe you were doing the dishes when you had that aha moment.

This is sometimes called the eureka effect—when you suddenly come to understand something that was previously incomprehensible. The legend goes that the ancient Greek scholar Archimedes had been struggling to determine how to measure an object's volume. But it wasn't until he stepped into his bath and saw the water level rise that he suddenly figured out how it could be done. He was so excited, he was said to have run naked through the streets shouting, "Eureka! I've done it!"

Similar stories of breakthrough revelations and sudden flashes of insight abound in myth and legend, as well as history. All, whether historical or mythological, tend to point to the remarkable fact that spontaneous solutions and insights often occur during periods of rest rather than strenuous effort. They remind us that we only need to present our mind with information, pose questions, and then rest until insight and realization naturally arise.

The fact is that when you effortfully strain to come up with new ideas, it's nearly impossible to produce anything brilliant. When you endlessly think about yourself and call it self-reflection, you end up moody and confused about what to do. It seems far more often that the solution arises whole and unbidden into your awareness only when you take a break to nap, go for a walk, play a game, engage in casual conversation with a friend, or spend time in the garden. It's only when you're just experiencing life in the moment that profound realizations spontaneously arise.

Another feature of these realizations is how distinctly "out of nowhere" and instantaneous they seem. Maybe one moment you saw someone as a friend and the next moment as something more. Or the opposite: one moment you're in love and the next moment you're not. One moment you don't know what school to attend, where to move, or which job to take, and the next moment you do.

And while you may argue that all your effortful thinking beforehand was critical to the manifestation of a spontaneous realization later on, the truth is that if you examine your experiences carefully, you'll realize that much of your thinking was extraneous to the process. Instead, the conditions you experience are always changing, and when the conditions align for you to think a new idea, receive a profound realization, or make an impactful decision, you spontaneously ideate, realize, and decide then and not a moment sooner—whether you spend hours pondering and agonizing over an issue . . . or not.

In other words, *you only need to know what you need to know when you need to know it, and not a moment sooner.* Much of your thinking is a vain attempt to know more than you need to know at that moment. When you stop trying to do that, you'll naturally know what you need to know right then and there.

The more you overthink the problem, the more you obscure the solution and confuse yourself further. We've all been there. Agitation caused by mental storytelling and anxious pondering over possible outcomes wastes a lot of valuable energy that could be used more effectively. Only when you disengage the mind's storytelling and come to rest in your default state of inner peace does the path suddenly become clear. From this vantage point, free of mental confabulation, you can see the present moment perfectly as it is and so you experience reality as it's really happening *before* your mind overlays stories on it. When you rest in the default peace state, you instantly become fully present.

Each time you disengage the mind, you experience a drop of inner peace dripping into your well. As you practice repeatedly returning in each new moment, you gradually fill your inner well of peace, little by little, drop by drop, until you're overflowing with fullness.

Presence, peace, and power are so closely intertwined that it is pretty much impossible to separate them. When you're at peace, you're present. When you're present, you're at peace. And power naturally follows where there's peace and presence. There are subtle differences between them, however, and it's helpful to know each in depth, but just bear in mind that when looking at peace versus presence or vice versa, it's not dissimilar to comparing facets of a single diamond.

So *peace* doesn't mean satisfaction with a particular situation but rather freedom from the stress of mental storytelling. *Presence* means being fully absorbed with what's happening here and now rather than dwelling on the past or worrying about the future. And *power* does not mean force, intense effort, or control over others, but rather the ability to know, say, or do whatever the moment demands. All together, these incredibly potent and life-changing forces conspire to create a life of meaning. And it all starts with peace.

And that leaves us with one question only: How does one cultivate inner peace? That may sound simple, and in one sense it is, but it's also challenging, because our minds and the societies we live in tend to work fairly tirelessly to distract us from exactly that. Luckily, there have existed throughout millennia traditions like shamanism that teach practices and ways of being that will set you on the path to inner peace.

Practices

Remember that peace is your default state. When you wake up in the morning, before your mind overlays stories onto reality, you are in a state of peace. Therefore, there really isn't anything you have to do to access this natural state . . . rather, there are some things you need to *not do*. You will need to learn how to *be* instead. Being and not-doing are the first and most central practice to this teaching because presence, power, and purpose naturally flow from them. If we can accomplish this step, the rest happens organically. If we can just *be* in each moment, we'll spontaneously *do*.

Not-doing might sound paradoxical, but it's simpler than it sounds. Remember how being at peace makes you present and vice versa? The two are inextricably woven into one thread. Therefore, to cultivate one is to experience the other. So when you focus on the present moment, you will find inner peace.

And here's the big secret: All your physical senses are gateways to the present moment. Sight, hearing, smell, taste, and touch are apertures through which reality flows into your awareness. When you draw your attention to any of these openings and become absorbed in the sensations there, you are, by definition, experiencing the present moment. That's because your physical senses are always happening *right now*.

So, let's give it a try.

Practice: The Peaceful Yawn

Wherever you are right now, spend a few minutes making sure you're comfortable—if you've been sitting and reading for a while, you may want to stand up and stretch a bit. When you sit back down, try your best to sit with your spine straight and your head balanced at the top of your spine.

Now take a long, slow, deep breath in, relishing the sense of expansion in the center of your body. Let the air inflate you like a balloon until your head rises slightly. Then open your mouth wide and exhale fully in surrender while yawning a long, "Ah," and relaxing your whole body. Savor the sensations arising in you. Pause here for a moment and notice the subtle bliss of reposing in your own being. You have nothing to do but this and nowhere to be but here.

As you sit, you might notice your mind becomes a little quieter or your thoughts slow down or stop as your attention is absorbed by physical sensation. See how long you can hang out in this space. And if you can, notice the moment when your thoughts reappear.

Even this simple yawning practice contains a droplet of true peace. Of course, as you rest in the afterglow of your peaceful yawn, you'll notice that the glow fades quickly at first. But if you practice repeatedly, eventually you'll find that the peace pervades your whole being and you'll find yourself constantly reposing in inner peace as an automatic habit. In fact, you could potentially practice only this mini meditation with regularity and, drop by drop, you would fill up your well of inner peace without needing any other practice—that's how powerful it is.

Try it one more time. Take another deep breath, fully expanding the belly, chest, and shoulders. Exhale fully and yawn a long "Ah" as you relax even further. Abide in the blissful sensations arising in your body for as long as you can. But don't be frustrated when the bliss fades. Notice how the bliss departs in direct relation to your mental monologue's return.

Congratulations! You've tasted a tiny morsel of inner peace, which you may visualize as a tiny seed of light within the center of your being. As you nurture it, it will only become stronger and stronger until you are continually moving through the world bathed in its light.

Let's go further now.

Practice: Centering in the Senses

Settle into a relaxed posture. Blink a few times and roll your eyes around. Now rest your eyes on any object before you—the farther away, the better. Loosen and widen your focus so that you're not concentrating on the object, but instead observing your entire field of vision. See the whole instead of focusing on any specific part. Imagine you're looking at a screen displaying a single image. Notice the colors vibrating before you. Notice how the image is constantly changing, mutating, shapeshifting.

If anything about your visual experience seems beautiful to you, indulge in that feeling of beauty. Abide in that feeling for as long as you can. Simply marvel at how spectacular your visual field really is and let yourself become absorbed in the colors and shapes. Notice the dreamlike quality of seeing.

When you're ready, let your eyelids get heavy and close, and shift your attention to your field of hearing. Listen to the entire sphere of sound surrounding you without focusing on any individual sound. As in the visual part of the exercise, observe the whole field of hearing as one object. In other words, listen to the symphony rather than any instrument in the orchestra.

You may notice a sense of expansion and clarity. For example, you might notice how the field of sound changes, mutates, and shapeshifts in much the same way as the visual field. You might begin to feel a sense of spaciousness by listening in this way, and you may be moved by what you hear. Let yourself become absorbed in the sounds and whatever feelings they spontaneously evoke. As you relax deeper into open listening, try to hear the deep bed of silence beneath all sounds. As you contemplate hearing the inaudible, as you try to listen to silence, your mind will go silent itself.

Next, and only when you're ready, shift your attention to your physical body. Scan your body for any tension. If you feel any tense muscles, take another deep breath. As you exhale, release the tension and let your whole body go limp. After a few deep breaths, notice the parts of your body that don't want to relax, that stay tense despite your intention. Let them be as they are while noting that the energy in that spot appears to be stuck.

As you relax in this conscious manner, energy bound up in your muscles releases and circulates throughout your body. You may feel this as warmth, tingling, or other bodily sensations. Enjoy all the sensations flowing through you from head to toe. Indulge in any pleasure you feel in the body. It feels good to have a body, so just enjoy the gift of your physical being.

If you get drowsy, that's a good sign that you're unwinding your mental monologue. But you do need to remain alert without dozing off, so when you notice drowsiness arising, take a deep breath in, hold the breath for a few seconds, and then exhale. You should notice a wave of energy reengage your mind.

Once you feel your time with your physical body is complete, bring your attention to the breath.

Notice your breath as it moves in and out through your nose. Notice how your belly and chest expand as you inhale. Notice your belly and chest contract as you exhale. Notice how inhaling feels empowering as you magnetically draw energy into your center. Notice how exhaling feels like surrendering as you release the breath and offer it back to the world. It feels good to breathe, so take a moment to really indulge; taking in what you need and releasing what you don't. Isn't it a blessing that whenever you feel a thirst for air, you need only inhale and your thirst is quenched? Find gratitude for the gift of each breath, and rest in that gratitude for as long as you can.

It's okay if thoughts are still arising. Just pay attention to the physical sensations in the body. The more you attend to your sensations, the less you can attend to your mental stories. Let them remain in the background.

Enjoy your breath for as long as you like. When you're ready to complete the exercise, take another long, slow, deep breath, letting your body fully expand. Then exhale with another "Ah." Then wiggle your toes, wiggle your fingers, and gently blink your eyes open. Notice the dreamlike quality of your surroundings. Notice the afterglow of your practice and notice how it fades as the mental monologue revs up.

Well done. You've completed your first two meditations, both of which cultivate the skill of turning to the present through the gateways of the senses. You've spent most of your life turning to the mind or heart as a reflexive reaction to changing circumstances. By constantly practicing turning to the present instead, you eventually find that being present becomes your reflexive reaction to every circumstance.

In difficult situations, we react reflexively. If we can return to the present moment, that allows us to act mindfully instead. The first two exercises are ways to center and ground ourselves because they bring us back to our literal center and ground us in the present moment. These exercises can be taken further so that you can practice cultivating inner peace all day, and not just when you're resting or meditating.

Practice: Peaceful Doing

We all must complete tasks each day that we might call boring or repetitive, such as washing the dishes or driving. In this practice, you'll try becoming utterly absorbed in that activity as you're doing it.

First, you'll want to make sure that you don't have any distractions. Don't multitask. Don't listen to music (unless that's the activity). Don't have the TV on in the background.

As you're washing the dishes, sweeping the floor, or performing another task that doesn't take a lot of mental energy, draw all your attention to the physical sensations of performing that activity. For example, focus on the hot water running over the dishes, the smoothness of the plates, and the scent of the dish soap or the way the broom glides across the floor and makes whatever shape you choose.

As you perform the activity with full undistracted attention, you'll become absorbed in it. The magical part is that you'll likely enjoy the activity on some level even if it's unpleasant. The enjoyment of the activity has nothing to do with how much you want to do it or not, but rather how fully you experience the activity while you're doing it.

Everyday activities offer an infinite abundance of sensory experiences for you to abide in, but you usually breeze past them without paying attention. Whenever you do abide in those opportunities, you are at peace even as you're engaging in activity. It is this internal peace that allows you to do the activity well. Any mental stories about the activity only create resistance or attachment.

All the practices above can be summed up in this simple instruction: *Delight in the fullness of each moment.* In any given moment, you're surrounded by opportunities to access the real here and now. Each moment is bursting with opportunities for sensory absorption, but we usually hang out in our heads all day instead. If we delighted in the richness of each sensory experience, when could we possibly feel empty?

The next time you're in a stressful condition—whether it's an internal mood or an external conflict—try returning to your physical sensations and especially your breath, which occurs literally at your core. Center yourself there and ground in the present moment. Then notice that whatever you need to know, say, or do to move through that moment spontaneously becomes clear. When no action is obvious, surrender the need to act.

Once you've worked with these exercises just a few times, you will understand that inner peace is always available to you via these sensory experiences. If you were to only do these first exercises, you could attain inner peace, which is the ground out of which grows outer power.

But now that you've learned how these forces work together and you've gotten a taste of the potential within the cultivation of peace and presence, let's take these ideas deeper. To fully utilize the personal power you will begin to experience more and more through the exercises above, you will need to understand how peace and power manifest in four key areas of your life: the body, the heart, the mind, and the spirit.

Learning how to find peace within these four major powers, and balance them properly, is critical for maximizing your power. If you let these four centers of power remain out of balance or misuse them, your ability to stay in the peace state may plateau or weaken, and you won't be able to reach your highest potential.

So let's dive in to examining each of these four major power centers, as well as how to align them and how to use them effectively. We'll begin with the body.

Chapter Two

Peace and Power in the Body

For many years, I had a tortuous relationship with my body. Born with a cleft lip, I endured multiple surgeries throughout childhood and struggled with a speech impediment. Growing up, kids never failed to remind me that I looked different from what was "normal." Even some adults would stare or do a double take.

Naturally, due to the messages I received from children and adults alike, I grew up believing I was ugly. I begged my parents for plastic surgery and prayed that God would magically transform me one day. I wanted so badly to look like someone else. After all, who would ever desire me? Who would ever love me? Bitter resentment and self-hatred festered inside me year after year. Filled with self-contempt, I abused my body by eating terrible food and not taking care of myself. I let my body deteriorate as I sank deeper into misery. I was often sick and frequently hospitalized. Altogether, I felt hopeless.

In what proved to be serendipitous, my own breakthrough regarding my struggle with my physical appearance came one day as I was having a mundane conversation with a close friend. As I was listening to her and studying her expression, her face suddenly seemed to transform into someone unrecognizable. Her features were the same, and yet I was seeing a completely different person looking at me. The French have a word for this phenomenon of suddenly seeing something familiar as totally unfamiliar: *jamais vu*, the opposite of déjà vu, which is suddenly seeing something totally unfamiliar as strangely familiar.

For one shining moment of clarity, I saw that faces are not static objects like fixed landscapes—they are ever changing, like waves on the ocean. No two people see one face the same way. Faces are like Rorschach inkblots: the way you see someone's face says more about you than them.

Realizing that my face was not a fixed object but a fluid energy, I sought to understand how I could utilize that energy. I quickly discovered that people with positive energy appear attractive regardless of their physical features, and people with negative energy appear unattractive regardless of how externally beautiful they may be. The more I focused on cultivating my own positive energy and attitude, the more people found me attractive. But it all started with me realizing that I didn't need to change my physical face; I needed to change my relationship with my body.

Shamanism and the Body

Shamanism teaches that the body is *not the essence of what you are*. It is simply the vehicle through which you are able to explore material reality.

You may consider your body to be the line where you stop and the world begins. But your body and the world are too intertwined to be separate things at all. You're not a solid object. You're a wave of energy.

Where is the boundary between your breath and the air? Your breath is probably the most intimate part of you, and yet it has no discernible border. So, while you're used to considering your sense of self to stop at your skin, the truth is that you have no physical boundary.

In the shamanic view, the nonphysical spirit emanates a physical body and not the other way around, just as the energy of a star produces the material elements. Spirit descends into bodily form the way lava cools to rock. Since all matter is just energy in a temporary physical state, that means you can see yourself equally as either a material or energetic being, depending on where you're directing your awareness.

By internalizing this understanding, we come to see that our body is neither the limit nor the essence of what we are. Most of us make the mistake of identifying solely with our body. The problem with this is that our body is impermanent. If your identity rests on your body, then as your youth wanes, your beauty fades, and your body decays, you'll be left with no support but terror, hopeless-ness, and powerlessness. That's no way to live. Loving and nourishing your body do not require identifying with it, as you can love and nourish a garden without becoming it.

When you realize that you are not just your body, you'll be less disturbed by the transformations your body will inevitably undergo. When you realize you are the greater natural process that's manifesting the entire cosmos—which your body is only a small portion of—you identify with and find support in that greater process instead of your body.

Still, you may cling to the notion that you are your body because that's what you've always been told. But how could you be your body if your body is constantly changing but the self you perceive yourself to be is not?

Your whole life, you have been yourself. And though your body has been changing the whole time, you're still consistently yourself. In fact, the molecules in your body are constantly reproducing and dying, so you're literally not in the same body you were born in. And yet, you are still fundamentally you on the inside. Sure, your personal-ity has grown and changed, you've learned lessons, you've matured. But the "I" inside you has remained inexplicably consistent. The unchanging "I," the part of you that wit-nesses the thoughts and feelings comprising your changing body and personality, is your spirit.

The universal experience of being a permanent self in an impermanent body reveals that your immaterial consciousness is more fundamental to your essence than your material body. One changes, the other doesn't. Identifying with the body traps you in believing you are a solid object rather than fluid energy.

The teaching here does not in any way denigrate the body or disparage it as impure. Quite the contrary: realizing the body is an expression of the universal consciousness elevates the body to its rightful place as an aspect of spirit, rather than a fallen creation or a mechanical system. When you come to see your body as an astonishing vehicle on magical loan from the cosmos, you can treat it with the proper respect it deserves. It's just that we want to properly contextualize the body as an impermanent aspect of our essential spirit, and not get caught thinking we are *only* a body.

Your body is quite literally a temple, as it's a temporary container housing the boundless spirit. Your consciousness is the divinity at the altar of the body temple.

Finding Peace in the Body

Cultivating peace in general is the key to outer power, but there are areas in which narrowing the scope of peace to explore specific issues and blocks can be helpful, and the body is definitely one of those areas in which nearly everyone can benefit from this inner work.

Peace can also be defined as *radical acceptance*—this sense of accepting whatever comes, whether good or bad, with the same level of readiness and equilibrium. Therefore, it makes sense that in order to fully empower the body, one must first pursue radical acceptance of the body as it is in the present moment.

Naturally, this is harder than it sounds! And don't get me wrong, I am not talking about acceptance as in, *Well, I have this body and I guess I have to accept it,* or *There's no point in trying to change anything about my body or improve my physical health because I have to accept it as it is.* Both of these approaches are infused with the same sense of defeat and resistance that drains our power in all aspects of our lives. Rather, the kind of acceptance I am talking about has to do with cultivating genuine gratitude for having a human body, for the miracle of its being. Shamanic traditions teach that each life-form on the planet is important and fulfills a purpose and a function. Of all the forms life takes on earth, you've been given a human one, and that is a tremendous gift.

Take a few moments right now to tune in to your physical body. There may be parts of your body that you believe are less than optimal—perhaps you've been told that parts of you are too big or too small, too wide or too narrow—take note of those feelings, but don't dwell on them. Simply let them go and feel them fade away into the air around you. You may also notice aches and pains that you've become accustomed to and now are making themselves particularly known. Likewise, acknowledge these (you might even say out loud, "Hello pain in my right knee"—sometimes giving voice to the thought can help in releasing it) and then let them go. You may still feel them, of course, but you are no longer concentrating on them. Now, just rest for a few moments in the realization that your body is miraculous—much of it working to keep you alive and breathing without any conscious effort—and see if you can feel gratitude for all that it does for you and with you on a daily basis.

This gratitude and radical acceptance of the body may take time, so don't beat yourself up if you find it difficult to overcome years of frustration with your body at first. One powerful ally in this journey of making peace with your body is a journal, which you can use to process all your thoughts, memories, and gratitude for your body regularly.

The more you work at cultivating peace in your physical body, the easier you'll find it will be to manifest personal power of the body on a regular basis.

Empowering the Body

The body accrues power—this is one of its primary reasons for being. When it is allowed to function at its highest levels, it can be compared to a beautiful, complex, spiritual battery. And it works best when approached in a spirit of balance. You can accrue power by nourishing the body with nutritious food, spending time outdoors, getting regular physical activity, and fostering meaningful relationships.

But you lose power when you mindlessly cave to your body's every desire. Your body wants to indulge, consume, and feel pleasure. But if you obey every bodily impulse to the point of excess, you'll find yourself always craving more and never being satisfied—to the point of imbalance and maybe illness. On the other hand, if you ignore your needs and neglect your body, a similar thing can happen: you'll feel unfulfilled in a different way, detached, and maybe depressed. Here's the thing: you must inhabit your body and listen to it while keeping in mind that it's not the only aspect of your full self—it's your job to balance these bodily needs, wants, and desires with what your mind and spirit want as well. Let's look at a few ways we can empower the body to serve us better.

Eat Good Food

We commonly lose power by eating food that lacks nutritional value, which forces the body to work harder digesting food that gives very little reward. Unhealthy food makes you lethargic, and habitually choosing to eat this way will always exacerbate a lack of power. You've probably already recognized that some foods make you feel good, while others don't. Every body is different, but most of us know which foods are not helpful to us personally. Focus on eating foods that energize you and that you love to eat, and avoid those foods that make you feel bad. It's almost as simple as that. If you follow this guidance, your body should be able to find balance, and you'll see that your appearance and weight will be happy afterthoughts—not a goal.

Recharge in Nature

Too much time spent indoors looking at screens depletes our energy. The body needs sunshine and fresh air, but also the sight and energy of trees, birds, and clouds far away. We spend so much time now staring at words up close that it's important to regularly step outside and look at how big and spacious the world really is. Nature is the ultimate power source, a recharging station for your body's battery, so indulge in it often. Make hiking trips a priority, eat a meal outside when you can, and explore the parks in your city and state. (I'll bet there are several within a short drive of you that you didn't even know existed!)

Move Your Body

The human body evolved to walk for dozens of miles at a time. We weren't made for the sedentary lifestyles that many of us find ourselves in today. The more active you are each day, the easier it is to remain active. The less active you are, the more difficult it is to get moving. Activity does not mean productivity, but literally moving your body. Even in our busiest of days, we can find ten minutes to do some yoga, take a brisk walk around the block, or dance with our kids after work. If you are able to build a committed exercise routine, that's amazing—and I don't need to tell you all the benefits of this. But be flexible and start small if you need to. Just move your body rather than not. Every day.

Cultivate Intimacy

You've probably had a friend whose thrilling, fast, sexy lifestyle seemed enviable. Their no-strings-attached sexuality may have come across as confident, and their devil-may-care attitude may have made them seem bulletproof. But when you connect with someone sexually, you exchange energy with them. And if that sexual interaction is only a physical transaction between your bodies, it will drain your energy. What may start as liberating exploration may soon leave you feeling lonely, lost, and used.

This is not to say that sex is bad, dirty, or sinful. There is enough shame surrounding sex in modern culture as it is—I am not suggesting we add to it! Savoring sex, passion, and love is an essential joy of life. But the sexual energy that drives us and the creative energy we use to manifest our intent are one and the same. If this energy moves in one direction, without including the reciprocity of intimacy in exchange, you will deplete it. This cosmic, potent power of creation—by which anything and everything is created—is precious. You can choose to engage in encounters that lack intimacy, but be aware of the energy you're spending and be ready to balance it out elsewhere.

In contrast, sex with intimacy is one of the most empowering activities available. We mistakenly associate the satisfaction of the sexual experience with the physical attraction to someone's body. In fact, the satisfaction comes from the spiritual, mental, and emotional connection more than the physical. When the physical activity is an expression of the deeper connection, sex becomes a magical fountain of power that charges you up on all levels.

$$\approx$$

In summary, be mindful of what you put in your body, where you go with your body, what you do with your body, and who you do it with. If you realize you're wasting power in these ways, you may feel overwhelmed or defeated—but that's only another waste of power. Instead, let's focus on gentler methods to create lasting change and increase power.

Transforming the Body

Chances are, you already know what you should do to take better care of your body, but you struggle to find the time or motivation to create new habits. If you can dispel the notion that your body is a static object and realize that it's constantly transforming energy, then change becomes a little more accessible. Since the body is changing constantly all the time, whether we consciously shape that change or not, then even small, positive adjustments will affect the outcome. That is, adding a green salad to your lunch or taking a thirty-minute walk outside when you'd rather catch up on social media can be small ways to shift the energy in your body—and over time, these small things add up.

The transformation I'm talking about here is toward health, power, and fullness, not about attaining some cultural standard of beauty. Real beauty naturally emanates when you're healthy and powerful. It's also important to keep in mind that the energy to transform the body is enhanced when you begin from a place of peace with your body as it is in the moment. Transformation should be about joy and never about self-recrimination.

Remember also that all of reality happens in the moment, not in the future, so material changes are always accomplished through actions here and now. Dramatic changes to our diet, routine, or habits often only bring temporary results. Such dramatic change may be necessary if you suffer from addiction and need to quit cold turkey, but that's why support is so crucial for recovery. Concerning individual self-improvement, you might lose weight, gain strength, or be healthier/happier for a brief period until you lose the energy to sustain such intense effort.

That means strategies involving calendar goals may not meaningfully change your underlying patterns enough to permanently transform your body. Forcing intense regimens to dramatically change your health may bring excellent short-term benefits and enhance your overall willpower, but they're not the best approach if you genuinely want to transform your body for good. You can plan to exercise more often or stop eating meat, but you cannot really guarantee your future self will fulfill any of those promises, thus setting yourself up for failure.

The only field of action we can really make a difference in is our daily cycle—and committing to improvement in the moment, since that's when change happens. Since controlling our diet and exercise is one of the most common obstacles to physical change, I'll use that as an example.

Practice: Gentle Intentions

Whether it's eating better or exercising more, set a gentle intention to do your best to eat something healthy the next time you're hungry or to exercise a little when you're tired. When hunger or weariness come around, do your best to follow through on that gentle intention. If you can't motivate yourself to follow through, then give yourself permission to eat what you want or lie around. But make sure to genuinely savor and enjoy that experience without any guilt or judgment. Simply reset the intention to try again at the next opportunity.

You may skip many opportunities to do your best. But I promise that after skipping just a few opportunities, you'll be tired of not doing your best and you'll discover motivation to do better. Whenever you do make a healthy choice, congratulate yourself with a feeling of pride for doing your best. This self-congratulation is the key to the practice.

The more often you congratulate yourself for making these small healthy choices, the more you'll train yourself to enjoy making such changes. Gradually, you'll find that doing your best in each moment becomes easier and easier.

Start with a goal that is within reach: for example, eating one healthy meal or going for a walk. When that reachable goal becomes a natural habit that you enjoy, choose the next reachable goal: for example, running instead of walking. Little by little, you'll transform your underlying habits and physical transformation will follow. Forcing yourself to do anything more than this simple practice will not guarantee lasting change.

When you set a calendar goal (such as losing weight by a certain date), you delay happiness until the date arrives. Until then, you practice enduring unhappiness, which is just practicing being unhappy. When the date arrives, even if you've attained the goal, you'll find yourself no happier than when you started. In fact, you'll find you somehow feel worse because you were expecting this accomplishment to fill the emptiness.

Here's the secret to this practice: By setting reachable goals that only look one meal or one walk ahead, you congratulate yourself more often. You practice being happy and victorious anytime, you simply do your best, so doing your best becomes joyfully addictive. You've then banished the problem of lacking motivation by rewiring your body to enjoy doing what you determine is best. Gradually, your body wants to eat better and exercise more, not because you're forcing it to, but because it's genuinely rewarding. You can (and should) be flexible about what eating better and exercising look like, as we all know that life has a way of interrupting our best intentions and plans—but what you can't skip is consistently providing that reward by congratulating yourself for doing your best whenever you can.

It's not only the accumulation of small habitual changes that makes a difference here. It's also the accumulation of pride in doing your best that further motivates you to do even better. The shame you feel after indulging a bad habit is the seed for the next craving, whereas the pride you feel after doing your best is the seed for the next healthy choice. That's the secret magic of this practice.

Practice: Making Offerings

Eating is not only about acquiring power. Eating is an opportunity to connect with nature, the ultimate power. You don't have to believe in a deity to be humbled by the awesome power of nature. You and the outside world are made of the same energy, and nowhere is that more obvious than when you eat something, transferring energy from one living thing to another.

All the food you eat is photosynthesized sunlight, so when I say you are a crystallization of energy that's not a metaphor. You are part of an endless natural cycle that includes the biosphere, the solar system, and the entire universe. It's easy to forget how profound the act of eating truly is, so we must practice remembering it. Making offerings is a shamanic way of connecting us to the deeper power of nature.

When you sit down to your next meal, don't devour it right away. Ground yourself with a deep, mindful breath, draw awareness to your belly, and acknowledge any hunger you sense there. Imagine this hunger is not just space in your belly, but a deeper emptiness within.

Now smell the aromas of your meal or admire its appearance on your plate. Let your mouth water and notice any other instinctual reactions in your body. As you take in the meal before you, remind yourself that this food is not only power, but a piece of the ultimate power of nature.

Give thanks, either silently or aloud, for the power you are about to receive. Honor the plants and animals you're consuming. Honor the people who prepared the food and everyone involved in bringing it to your plate, including the people who grew and raised the food. Honor the sun, soil, wind, and rain necessary to create you and the food which sustains you. Bless the food, making it sacred by acknowledging its connection to the greater natural cycles.

Make an offering. Take a small portion of your meal (even just a pinch of bread is fine) and say, either silently or aloud, that you offer this food back to the ultimate power from which it came, in grateful acknowledgment and humble reverence of this greater power. A small offering of water to a houseplant or a few crumbs for the birds outside the window works. Remember, your intent is what matters—the acknowledgment of the sacred nature of food and your remarkable relationship with the natural world. Offerings are symbols—they signal that you understand your reciprocal energetic relationship with the source of all power.

Once you've made your offering, slowly eat that first bite, savoring the sumptuous taste, texture, and temperature of the food, relishing in its deliciousness. Close your eyes to become fully absorbed in each eruption of flavor. After swallowing, draw your attention to the food moving down your central channel. As the food hits your stomach, indulge in the satiation of your hunger. Notice how the rest of your physical experience seems to brighten as the power of the food becomes yours.

Imagine the food is not only satiating your physical hunger, but also that the ultimate power is filling the existential emptiness within you. Abide in that satisfaction for as long as you can, and then enjoy your meal as usual. Occasionally experiment with maintaining this kind of awareness through eating an entire meal and discover how deeply nourishing mindful eating can be.

This simple practice continually reminds you of your interconnectedness with the power of nature. The more you treat the food you consume in this sacred manner, the more it will empower you. The more you make offerings in grateful acknowledgment of your borrowed power, the more power you can borrow. Because you will form a recip-rocal relationship with your environment, you will feel fur-ther empowered by your environment.

In a greater and more global sense, offerings can and should also be made in a more charitable manner. Regular donations to or volunteering at food banks will add even greater power to your practice. When you become comfort-able giving away a pleasurable necessity like food, you can't be ruled by food or cravings in general, and you'll feel more connected to the wider community and world. When you give away a little more money than you're comfortable with, and then you don't miss it later, you'll feel a deeper sense of abundance. Food and money can be seen as embodying similar principles: Both are a form of energy, both can be shared. Both can be approached in a spirit of scarcity and possessiveness or a spirit of generosity and flow.

Developing Physical Awareness

The body contains millions of nerves that radiate an infi-nite amount of sensory data. If you want to master your body and maximize its power to your advantage, you must become intimately familiar with the energy within it. The more you develop awareness within your body, the better you'll be able to forge a deep relationship with your body, its needs, and its abilities.

These days, we practice strengthening our muscles with tension and stretching, but we don't practice relaxing nearly enough. That's why we're not particularly good at it. Through the practice of intentional relaxation, you'll cultivate the physical ground of inner peace and calm that you can retreat to whenever you need. Your body is at its most powerful when you're relaxed. Even and especially when performing a strenuous physical task, the more relaxed you are, the more powerful you'll be.

Physical and mental relaxation go hand in hand. When you relax your body, your mind follows. It's easier to relax the body than the mind, so you can use the body to direct the mind to relax.

By regularly practicing relaxing, you'll develop the ability to relax your body even during crisis. When we perceive danger, our body produces adrenaline, which causes muscle tension. But here's a secret: your body can only produce stressful emotions when your muscles are tensed. The tension in the muscles produces adrenaline and cortisol, the stress hormone. When muscles release tension, your body feels safe and releases the pleasure hormones instead. As soon as you deliberately relax your muscles in a tense situation, you'll find your stress response relaxes too. Put simply, your body cannot produce negative emotions when your body is relaxed. Muscle tension = stress response; muscle relaxation = pleasure response.

When you're in a situation that has you reacting emotionally, mindfully encourage your body to relax so you can regain your wits. By regularly practicing the following grounding exercise and cultivating physical awareness, you'll be able to remain grounded more easily throughout your day, no matter what life throws at you.

Practice: Body Scanning

To start, relax into a comfortable seat. Try to sit up straight if you can. Feel free to lean against a chair or wall, or even practice lying down.

Take a deep breath in through the nose and out through the mouth. Inhale fully again, and then exhale fully. Take one more deep breath in through the nose, sip in a little extra air, and hold the breath to a count of five. Exhale, fully emptying the lungs.

Take another big breath in, but this time deliberately tense all your muscles: clench your fists, flex your abs, scrunch your face, etc. Squeeze your muscles until you're trembling, and then relax and exhale. We tense our muscles here to burn off extra energy. Try it a few times.

Settle back into your body as the tension you stirred up fades. Notice that you can relax a little deeper now. Observe the energy released from your muscles. Muscle tension is bound-up energy, so whenever you relax your muscles, you can feel energy releasing and circulating around your body.

Imagine a warm white fire kissing your feet and melting away the tension there. Let the feet relax as much as you can. Notice any tension in your feet that doesn't want to release, and just let it be there. Be curious about it. What is that muscle holding on to?

Draw your attention up to your calves. Imagine the warm white fire melting away the tension in the calves, letting them totally relax and noticing any tension that doesn't want to let go.

Now draw your attention up to your thighs. Imagine the warm white fire melting away the tension in the thighs, letting them totally relax and noticing any tension that doesn't want to let go.

Let your legs go totally limp. You might notice that your feet relax more deeply as your calves and thighs relax. Let your limp legs sink into the earth. Indulge in any pleasure you feel in your relaxed legs. You might notice tingling energy sensations as tension is released from your muscles.

Draw your attention up to your hips and hands. Imagine the warm white fire melting away the tension in the hips and hands, letting them totally relax and noticing any tension that doesn't want to let go.

Draw your attention up to your abdomen, lower back, and forearms. Imagine the warm white fire melting away the tension in the abs and lower back, letting them totally relax and noticing any tension that doesn't want to let go.

Draw your attention to your chest, upper back, upper arms, and shoulders next. Imagine the warm white fire melting away the tension in the chest, upper back, upper arms, and shoulders, letting them totally relax and noticing any tension that doesn't want to let go.

Now your whole body from the neck down should be limp and totally relaxed. Imagine you're sinking into the bosom of the earth. Notice how your limbs relax even further. Indulge in the pleasure of a relaxed body. You might notice tingling sensations throughout your body as your muscles release tension.

Draw your attention up to the neck and throat. Imagine the warm white fire melting away the tension in the neck and throat, letting them totally relax and noticing any tension that doesn't want to let go.

Draw your attention up to your face. Imagine the white fire melting away the tension in your face, letting your jaw, lips, eyes, and brow totally relax and noticing any tension that doesn't want to let go. It's normal for your eyes to flutter.

Draw your attention up to the top of your head. Imagine the white fire shooting out of your crown up to the sky.

Finally, imagine the white fire covering your entire body from head to toe. Rest here in this state of perfect relaxation and enjoy the pleasure surging through your body. Use your curiosity to drive your awareness, keenly observing the sensations running through you.

You may notice that there's still some lingering tension in your body. That's okay. It's just evidence that you've been unconsciously holding on to tension for ages. With practice, you'll find you can relax deeper and faster. And there are other methods for releasing tension that we'll look into as well. For now, just gently encourage your muscles to let go and then observe whatever sensations arise.

Let go of the fire visualization, letting it fade.

Now imagine that a pitcher of cool, clear water has been poured over your head. Imagine the cold splash on your crown. Imagine the cool, clear water surging down your brow, eyes, lips, and jaw. Observe the sensations coursing through your face.

Let the cool, clear water stream down your neck and throat and cascade across your shoulders. Feel the water flowing down your arms, through your forearms, and out your hands. Feel the water flowing from your head down into your chest, your belly, and your hips. Feel the water flowing into your thighs, down into your calves, and out your feet. Bask in the rich stream of sensations coursing through your whole body.

Repeat the process if you like, once again imagining warm white fire rising up from feet to crown and clear cool water pouring down from crown to feet. The more times you repeat the cycle, the more you'll intensify your awareness of the energetic sensations within you.

If you're performing the practice while lying down at bedtime, you can enjoy the feeling of relaxation until drowsiness arises and then surrender to sleep. But otherwise, you can finish your session by taking three more deep breaths in through the nose and out through the mouth and holding the breath to a count of five after the last inhale. As you exhale completely, wiggle your fingers and toes. Gently blink your eyes open. You might be a little dizzy or light-headed, so be careful as you get up.

This practice increases your physical awareness by circulating your attention through your nervous system, stimulating each nerve and encouraging it to send you more sensory data. Just as we work out a muscle to make it stronger, we can also use the nervous system to make it more sensitive.

With clearer, more radiant physical awareness, you'll be able to intentionally relax even in stressful conditions. Over time, this relaxed response to intense situations becomes reflexive and habitual. A warrior must be totally relaxed in order be fully aware of the moment and respond properly to it. Tension makes us jumpy, prone to hesitation or overreaction. By cultivating awareness, you'll have the calm patience of a true warrior.

As I developed my own physical awareness, I learned to just enjoy being in my body. I became more sensitive to how different foods, activities, and people made me feel. Through setting gentle intentions, I gradually improved my habits for a healthier lifestyle.

Rather than accept my body's limitations, I worked on expanding my abilities. I practiced shamanic and yogic breathing exercises to strengthen my respiratory system and enliven my energy body. With increasing power, I engaged in more physically demanding practices like postural yoga, aikido, and jujitsu. I sang and danced—some of the oldest and most powerful medicine. Over time, my breath steadied, my body strengthened, and I banished the demon of self-hatred.

Using Body Power

Now you know some ways to enhance your body power by making changes through gentle intentions, giving offerings that remind you of your connection to the greater natural cycle, and developing the physical awareness that allows you to feel energy and relax into peace. You also know the common ways you lose your power and how to contain it. But when you feel your newfound physical power blooming, how should you use it?

Physical power should be used to provide, protect, and preserve. Physical power is meant to create and nurture, not destroy and dominate.

We can look around the world today and see many examples of power being used to destroy nature and dominate people. To foster a better world, you need to learn how to create what is good and nurture it. Power is about protecting oneself and others and not simply defeating adversaries. The happy warrior does not just fight the bad but also builds and defends the good.

Of course, it's incredibly easy to feel hopeless in the face of the world's overwhelming array of problems. How can you, a single individual, make a meaningful difference through your small actions? But the truth is that it's never been easier for the individual to impact the whole. For all its faults, modern society affords us the magical ability to communicate globally. You can use your voice to speak out for what you believe. You can connect with other like-minded people as well as engage your adversaries.

You can act further by participating in local and national organizations that are already tackling the challenges you care about. You can use your civic and political power if you choose. Become present and determine what you can do here and now. Practice exercising your power. Even though you may not be physically fighting the dominating forces you oppose, you can still apply the principles of using your power to nurture and protect as you engage the sociopolitical domain.

≈

Accrue body power by eating nutritious food, spending time outdoors, staying physically active, and being intentional about who you share your energy with. Set gentle intentions to make small changes in each moment and you'll gradually transform your body in a joyful manner in a way that lasts. Make offerings to connect your body to the greater cycle of nature. Cultivate physical awareness to form a better relationship with your body.

Following these guidelines develops your ability to relax into your body at any moment, even and especially in stressful situations. Keeping your poise is crucial to acting with power. The happy warrior's secret to handling every situation mindfully is remembering to relax into their body and find the calm of inner peace first.

Chapter Three

Peace and Power in the Heart

For as far back as we have written records, the heart has been considered the nexus of love, feelings, passion, and intuition. The ancient Egyptians considered the heart the keeper of our moral and emotional selves and preserved the hearts of the deceased in ritual jars to accompany them on their journey through the underworld, where they would be asked to weigh that heart against the feather of divine harmony. Greek and Roman philosophers taught that the heart was the center of the soul and that it had a physical effect on a person's emotional reactions.

The connection between the heart and our emotions is evident in the cultural beliefs of today. When we experience a breakup or encounter something overwhelmingly sad, we are "heartbroken." We tell people to "listen to their heart" when making an important decision. We swear allegiance and loyalty by holding our hands over our hearts. No matter the origin of the concept, the heart remains the symbolic seat of the emotional body.

And yet, while all that the heart represents is still critical to living a life of passion and signifying the emotional part of ourselves, it's simultaneously true that our hearts are not the essence of who we are. While it's easy to mistakenly identify the self with the body, it's even easier to identify with your emotions. Identifying with the heart means believing that you *are* your feelings.

For example, when you say things like, "I am angry, I am sad, I am happy," you are taking ownership of these feeling as if they *are* you; but they aren't. Feelings are waves of emotional energy that pass through you. Everyone shares a collective pool of emotional energy, and we pass feelings back and forth and down through generations. Just as your body's cells turn over every several years, your emotions cycle even faster, within weeks, days, and hours.

In this swirling pool of emotional energy, it's easy to assume that every feeling is accurate and deserving of equal attention. But this distorts reality and makes it simpler to become ruled by emotion. You become emotion*al*. You lash out or retreat in ways that are destructive. You may end up blurting out hurtful words you don't mean or fail to say what's truly in your heart. Or you hesitate to stand up for what's right. If you identify too closely with every feeling that moves through you, you'll be more prone to being pulled away from your inner ground of peace. Yes, sometimes you'll be overcome with a feeling and can do nothing more than experience it fully. But in times of stress or conflict, when you need to keep your wits about you, your mood can sabotage you.

It can therefore be incredibly empowering to realize that it is not necessary to react fully to every emotion we may experience. Of course, I don't mean you should ignore or suppress your feelings. Rather, be fully aware of them in any given situation but then react intentionally from your spirit. Your emotions are real and important. You should feel, hear, and digest them fully. But trouble arises when you become absorbed *exclusively* in your emotions.

Cultivating Peace in the Heart

When you get swept away in an emotion—no matter how justified—your power drains into the emotional wave and this leads you to act unmindfully. Rage or speechlessness may be the appropriate emotional result of an insult or attack, but your ability to react or fight back depends on keeping your cool. If you've ever wished you had said something differently in a situation, then you know what it means to be swept away by your feelings. Just as obeying your body's every whim can set you on an imbalanced course, so too can obeying your heart's every whim. In essence, you become a slave to your mood.

Calming techniques for the body such as those we explored in chapter 2 will help you settle your feelings in the moment. But sometimes, as happens to all of us now and then, you may be overcome with emotions that agitate you physically. Your skin gets hot, your knees get wobbly, your stomach ties in knots. It's therefore helpful to have methods on hand to cultivate emotional calm *in conjunction* with physical calm. The two practices are mutually supportive, each making the other easier and more fruitful.

Just as you can lack awareness of your body, you can also lack awareness of your emotions. Ironically, being unaware of your heart makes you more susceptible to letting your heart lead you, because your reality is distorted by your emotional lenses without you even realizing it. Peace in the heart begins with developing our emotional awareness.

Practice: Opening the Heart

To begin, sit up comfortably with a straight back. Use pillows, a chair, or the wall to support you as needed. Take a few deep, yawning breaths to get centered.

Inhale and draw attention into your body, scanning for any muscle tension. As you exhale, release as much tension as you can.

Resume normal breathing. Delight in the fullness of each breath, savoring how it feels throughout your body. Imagine the air around you is a glimmering cloud of energy that you're drawing in with each breath. Try to feel the energy, the power, that enters you with each inhale.

Draw your attention into your central column: the belly, chest, and head. As you inhale, notice the pleasant sense of expansion in your center. As you exhale, notice the gentle contraction. On the next inhale, deliberately expand your belly and chest even more, inflating yourself like a balloon. As you exhale, deliberately contract inward, flexing your abs in toward the spine to fully empty the lungs. Breathe intentionally deep for a few rounds, and then resume normal breathing. Notice how each breath is a bit fuller, longer, and slower now.

Now scan your heart. Do you feel any emotional charge? Observe the sensations in your central column without judgment. If you were to only practice scanning your heart repeatedly throughout the day, you would develop extraordinarily sensitive emotional awareness.

Since you're reading quietly, you may have found that just returning to your center has brought about some emotional calm. But there is still likely a subtle emotional charge to this current experience. For example, if a distraction is annoying you, work with the sensation of annoyance.

If you can sense any emotional charge whatsoever, then the second step is labeling the emotion. Do your best to put a specific name to the feeling. Naming the emotion identifies it as something other than you. Every magico-spiritual tradition agrees that knowing something's name gives you power over it, so we're applying that concept to emotions.

As soon as you label the emotion, you may notice the feeling change. Maybe it relaxes or disappears altogether. Sometimes, just identifying the emotion is enough to dissipate its charge.

If you continue to feel the labeled emotion, you may notice thoughts such as, "I am sad, I am angry, I am lonely." The third step is to intentionally rephrase these sentences to make them more accurate: "I am not sad, there is sadness; I am not angry, there is anger; I am not lonely, there is loneliness." Having identified the emotion, take a moment to affirmatively repeat these statements to yourself: "I am not [the feeling]; there is [the feeling]." By removing the first person from these emotional sentences, you'll further break the habit of identifying with feelings.

As soon as you rephrase these sentences, you may notice the feeling change. Again, maybe it relaxes or disappears altogether. Sometimes, just rephrasing our inner narrative is enough to dissipate the emotional charge.

If you continue to feel the rephrased emotion, the fourth step is locating the emotional charge as a physical sensation in your body and then flooding that area with attention. For example, you might feel the emotion as a pit in your stomach, a knot in the chest, or a lump in the throat. Wherever you feel it, draw your attention there. As you inhale, imagine sucking white light energy from the air around you into that spot of your body, burning away the emotion. As you exhale, imagine the emotion is black smoke and blow it away. Notice how just imagining light coming into the body prompts physical sensations in that area. Notice how breathing energy into and out of that area discharges the emotion.

Finally, let go of the emotion and draw your attention to your heart center at the middle of your sternum. Feel the sensations in this area. If you can't feel much there, then your heart awareness is limited and your heart may be blocked. You can place your index finger or palm on your heart center to help bring awareness there.

As you inhale, feel the heart center expanding. As you exhale, feel it contracting.

Now, imagine you're a star. As you inhale, imagine your gravity is sucking energy into your heart center. As you exhale, imagine your starlight is shining back outward in all directions. Visualize a tiny green ball of light in the heart center. Breathe in, drawing energy into the sphere of light. Breathe out, letting the sphere grow larger. Slowly, breath by breath, inflate the green ball of energy until it fills the whole chest. Delight in any happy feelings that emerge from this visualization.

Keep breathing energy into the green ball and shining light outward, expanding the sphere until it fills your whole body. Delight in any happy feelings that pervade your body as you feel the green energy tingling within you. Keep inflating the green sphere until it fills the whole room. Feel the love in your heart expanding. Intentionally generate the emotion of love and happiness in the green light and throughout your body. Just as you can control your breath when you want, you can generate specific emotions when you want. Deliberately conjure as much joy as you can, even if you're pretending.

Then let the green sphere expand beyond the room and imagine it extending through the entire cosmos. Gradually, let the expanding green light dissipate. Drop all intentional breathing. Just relax into your body and rest. Repose in the afterglow of the practice, noticing a lightness in the heart and perhaps even a spark of joy. Stay here as long as you like, sealing in the work.

When you're ready, gently return to the world while doing your best to maintain this emotionally light but energetically full heart.

By regularly practicing this heart-opening technique, you'll cultivate clear emotional awareness, break your habit of identifying with every feeling, and banish negative emotional charge. Paying attention to the feelings in your body stimulates deeper emotional awareness. Labeling the emotions and removing the first person from the experience breaks the habit of identification. And flooding emotionally charged areas with attention, breath, and light dissipates the charge.

Practice each of these steps as often as necessary. Draw attention to your emotional body throughout the day and label the feelings that pass through the heart. Notice when you identify with your emotions and reframe things by removing the first person. And when you're feeling overwhelmed in a situation, pause to shine energy inward and regain your wits.

The more often you practice these simple exercises, the more effectively you'll be able to maintain your inner peace and keep your cool in any situation. Eventually, you find these practices become your new habits. Then, you always have awareness of your feelings and can clearly digest and articulate them. You won't take ownership of your emotions and mistake them for reality. Emotions will pass through you rather than consume you. When you experience difficult emotions, you'll know exactly how to digest and release them. By deliberately practicing generating happy emotions, you'll access deeper and deeper states of happiness and find that you can slip into happiness more easily more often.

Unlocking the Heart's Power

Emotions are like alarm bells going off inside your body. Pay close attention to the warning, but remember that you can choose how you will react. Will you freak out or will you remain calm? If you can remain calm, you're more likely able to get out of the metaphorical burning building safely and confidently—and you're more likely to help others get out too.

You can develop the ability to remain calm by cultivating emotional awareness. You can let go of your feelings by digesting them and moving on. You can express what your heart demands, and you can unlock the magic of speaking your heart. In other words, you'll be openhearted and well on your way to becoming a happy warrior.

By giving your feelings less authority to dictate your actions, your anger, depression, and helplessness can transform into passion, contentment, and power. Your heart becomes full rather than heavy. You're able to love yourself more genuinely. You're able to love others unconditionally without expecting anything in return. You'll be able to love because it feels good to share love and not for any other reason.

Aligning your heart does not mean that you're liberated from pain and sorrow. You'll still cry amid heartache and weep for tragedies near and far. Mastering your emotions does not make you a cold, unfeeling person. On the contrary, it makes you more emotionally sensitive. But you'll be able to digest the difficult emotions the same as the pleasant ones. And when difficult emotions arise, you won't be consumed by them even when you feel them fully.

The practices in the previous chapter taught you how to train your body to relax. The practices earlier in this chapter taught you how to digest your emotions fully by identifying, locating, and energizing them. If you practice these methods repeatedly, you'll find that giving your feelings away is easy. No matter how intense an emotional experience becomes, you'll be able to digest it and then let it go.

But sometimes, letting go isn't enough to give the feeling away. Some feelings need to be expressed. That expression can happen simply by writing the feeling down. But often, the feeling demands to be expressed to someone else. We long to confess our love, confront our adversaries, or speak our truth in some other important way, and until we do, we can't let the feeling go.

When you express your feelings aloud, the emotional energy moves up from your heart and out through your throat and mouth. When you silence your truth, the emotional energy sinks into your belly and groin, becoming latent time bombs of desire that can erupt unpredictably.

If you harbor guilt for a mistake, then you must confess it to let it go. If you're hiding romantic feelings for someone, then you must tell them before you miss the chance. If you're holding anger toward someone, you need to express that anger to heal from it. If you have strong feelings about how to make the world better, you must share them. If you miss the opportunities to confess, express, and share, then those emotions will stay bound in you forever. Only by speaking these feelings aloud can you truly give them away.

Notice that the freedom here comes from the expression itself, and not its result. Confessing your guilt may lead to punishment or retribution. Telling someone you love them might lead to rejection. Telling someone why you're angry may irreparably change or end a friendship. Sharing your opinions to the world may lead to criticism and attack. The outcomes are not up to you. Share your feelings simply to get them off your chest, and don't expect a particular result from your action other than letting the feeling go. You'll feel relief regardless of the outcome.

That doesn't mean we should indiscriminately share every feeling with everyone all the time. As I said above, most feelings can be digested without doing anything more than identifying and paying attention to them. Only some feelings demand expression. Those feelings will be obvious to you when you repeatedly try to let them go but they keep returning. Once you recognize that a chronic feeling must be expressed, you can purposefully determine what to say, who to say it to, how to say it, and when.

Only by sharing feelings can we experience the healing magic of heart power. Sharing your feelings does not mean angrily yelling at someone, but calmly articulating how you feel. When you can calmly express your most volatile emotions, you can fall in love, resolve conflicts, and make a difference in the world.

Practice: Recapitulation

Most daily emotions can be cleared through the practices already given. But emotions connected to trauma are not so easily healed. Just as your physical body can become injured, broken, and scarred, so too can your emotional body. Daily aches and pains can be treated with exercise and stretching, but serious injuries require time and attention to heal. So too with the heart.

Some experiences are traumatic, which in shamanic terms means they're too emotionally intense to digest while they occur or even long after. Your tension response to the traumatic experience becomes encoded into your muscle memory, causing you to habitually respond to minor stress with intense emotion. In other words, you experience post-traumatic stress.

The PTSD we associate with shell-shocked soldiers and victims of abuse is the most extreme example. But we all carry some form of trauma. For some of us who've been abused or suffered great tragedy, we know exactly how we've been traumatized. For some of us who are simply lost in life, we may not be sure what past traumas are blocking us.

Recapitulation is the practice of reclaiming the power we've lost in our traumatic experiences. When we get upset and hold on to that feeling, we continually get more upset as our trauma is triggered over and over. Through recapitulating our negative experiences, we can reclaim the power lost and drain those painful memories of any emotional charge.

To begin, sit comfortably with your back straight. Take a few mindful breaths as you relax your body. Scan for any tension and release it. Draw attention to your breath and just breathe for a few minutes until you feel rested but alert.

Choose a recent difficult memory to focus on. Remember it in all its detail and allow it to upset you. Notice how the emotional charge feels and locate it in your body as a physical sensation. Is the emotion felt as a lump in the throat, tightness in the chest, butterflies in the stomach, tension in the head, or shaking in the hands? Wherever you feel it, just observe it with curiosity.

Now reverse the memory. Imagine the memory is going backward, as if you are rewinding a movie. This can be challenging, so do your best and be patient with yourself. Eventually, you'll be able to visualize the memory in reverse. You may already feel the emotional charge lessening.

Now go back and forth, viewing the memory chronologically, and then in reverse, and then chronologically again. Be patient and gentle with yourself as you visualize this.

Once you can remember the memory going back and forth, then you are ready to reclaim the power and release the emotional charge.

Inhale through your nose, turn your head to the left, while imagine sucking the color out of the memory until it is black and white. Then exhale through your mouth as you turn your head to the right and imagine blowing the memory away like dust. Repeat this three times until you've completely blown the black-and-white memory away.

Now look straight ahead as you recall the memory in full color again. Do you still feel an emotional charge? If so, then repeat the process for this memory again. Continue repeating this process until you can remember the memory without any emotional charge.

Once you can recall the difficult memory without triggering an emotional charge, you have successfully recapitulated that event. Then, you're ready to recapitulate an earlier difficult memory. In this manner, gradually work your way backward, recapitulating every difficult memory from your life.

In one session you might recapitulate several minor incidents. Or a particularly deep trauma could take several sessions to recapitulate. Either way, patiently work through the practice while enjoying the fact that you're finally tackling your inner demons. Take pleasure in the process without rushing to the finish line. You can recapitulate as a daily practice to regularly discharge built-up emotional energy, and especially after stressful situations with a lingering emotional charge.

Through recapitulation, you can heal your heart's deeper wounds and reclaim the power bound up in your trauma. Recapitulation is a somatic form of self-therapy. In shamanic terms, you're digesting the emotion and reclaiming its power. In psychological terms, you're repeatedly but gently reexposing yourself to the traumatic event until you become desensitized.

Using the Heart Power

I once worked with an incredible singer named Elizabeth who was losing her voice right as her career was taking off. The year before, she had signed a record deal and recorded an album. But in the weeks leading up to her first world tour, her voice failed her. She visited the best doctors, but no one could find anything wrong with her vocal cords. She'd desperately tried every remedy available, but she still couldn't sing. She was understandably terrified that she was going to miss her moment.

As I sat with Elizabeth, I learned that she was brought up with a deeply religious worldview but had realized a long time ago that she didn't believe in it anymore—and she'd never told anyone in her family or community. Elizabeth feared her family's reaction to the news, of course, but she also believed that spirituality wasn't worth making a fuss over. So she spent her time focusing on her career without ever needing to rock that particular boat.

The problem was instantly clear: Elizabeth was about to unveil her persona to the world, but she was still hiding her real self. By pretending to be a believer, she never said what she truly believed. Her truth was stuffed deep down inside her heart. She couldn't sing because she refused to speak her truth.

I guided Elizabeth to begin a gradual process of "coming out" as a nonbeliever. Tailored to her specific situation, the process began with sharing her real beliefs with trusted friends and gradually moved outward to difficult family members, and then eventually to her wider community. Naturally, not everyone agreed with her opinions—and she did need to develop clear and strong boundaries with difficult family members—but the overwhelming majority of people in her community supported her decision to be honest about who she was.

And, tellingly, the more authentically Elizabeth behaved—in line with her own beliefs—the more her voice returned. Especially after confronting her family and revealing her "secret" to them, her voice roared back to life. By the time she went on tour, her vocal power was second only to her power of self-expression.

If the body's reason for being is accruing physical power, then the heart's reason for being is giving emotional burdens away. Whereas you should hold on to your physical power and give it away sparingly, you should give away your emotional power freely and avoid holding on to it. In the simplest terms, giving away your feelings means letting them go. Once an emotional experience has been fully expressed, processed, and digested, the happy warrior releases the emotion and moves forward unburdened.

For example, someone may do something disharmonious that makes you feel anger, which is a perfectly legitimate response in any number of situations. If you can experience the anger and let it go in that moment, then you can clearly and mindfully respond to the situation.

We often hold on to anger even after the situation that triggered it has passed. The longer you hold that anger, the worse it becomes, devolving into bitterness and resentment that taints your reality. Gradually, you find yourself angry at everything and everyone, and you find more and more reasons to be angry. More negative experiences accumulate around you, constantly triggering more anger. What starts off as a moment of anger eventually twists you into an angry person.

Emotions are energy passing through us. We shouldn't hold on to this energy but allow it to pass. When we resist an emotion, we don't digest its energy properly and bind it up in our bodies as physical tension instead. For example, even when you feel just a little bit of stress, your shoulders tense and shrug upward. But the reverse is also true. If you can intentionally relax the shoulders, the feeling of stress also relaxes. Emotional tension causes physical tension and vice versa.

That tension flares up again and again, and until you can digest the emotion fully, the bind deepens. Eventually, your shoulders don't just tense up when you're stressed— they stay tense all the time, causing pain and possibly health problems.

Cultivating Compassion

As I recapitulated my own past traumas, the emotional energy bound up in my resentment and anger dissipated. Day after day, I reviewed my most difficult memories and methodically reclaimed my power from each one. Some memories released in mere minutes, while others took many months. But little by little, my heart lifted and shone brighter until the black hole itself was a distant memory.

Once I was able to view my emotions as energy, I felt them as vibrations rather than moods. It became easier to let my emotions come and go like clouds in the sky. I stopped taking my feelings so seriously all the time, so they stopped feeling so serious.

As I released my past traumas and refused to identify by them anymore, I shed my old identity as a weak, sick, and sad child. I shed my attachment to the idea of being an artist or anything else. In letting go of any expectations of who I should be, I was finally able to be truly myself. Even better, I was able to allow all aspects of myself to shine through rather than be limited by a single identity.

As I awakened emotionally, I practiced sharing my feelings. For so long, I'd nursed my wounds as my own dirty secrets, keeping them hidden and letting them fester unseen. But now, as I reclaimed my emotional power, I was able to express my feelings freely. To my amazement, the more openly I shared my feelings, the more people responded to me positively and saw me as confident, not weak. I realized that showing my vulnerability was the best demonstration of strength.

Although my heart was changing, the world remained the same frustrating, unjust mess. Rage remained in me, but it no longer ruled my heart. Compassion took over. When I saw the suffering in the world, I felt love and compassion for people, animals, and nature. Rather than feeling powerless, I found outlets to share my feelings and forged connections with other like-minded people. By remaining in the present moment, I focused on taking small tangible acts here and now rather than trying to save the world.

Fiery anger was wiped out by cool compassion. Just as peacefully returning to my breath became my default reaction to any stressful condition, so too did compassion become my default response to anger. Before, I was drowning in a sea of tumultuous feelings. Now, I've built myself a little boat to brave the waves.

Remember, walking with an open heart will not make you a pushover. In fact, it will give you strength to do the right thing in every moment. Being openhearted means understanding your suffering enough to feel others' suffering as your own and then doing something about it. It does not mean you are unemotional, but that you are comfortable with all emotions because you know they are all temporary. Only when you express your darkest feelings and release them can you be a true friend, lover, and healer. Until then, you're only ever preoccupied with your own pain. Your feelings need not define you since you get to define your feelings.

So far, we've learned that you are not just your body, but that your body is a material extension of your true immaterial self. You've learned that you are not your feelings either, since feelings are just passing through you. Even your feelings are a material extension of your true immaterial self, but subtler than the physical body.

But even when your body is strong and your heart is open, it does you no good if you let your mind run amok. So let's get explore peace and power in the mind next.

Chapter Four

Peace and Power in the Mind

Nan-in, a Japanese master during the Meiji era (1868–1912), received a university professor who came to inquire about Zen.

Nan-in served tea. He poured his visitor's cup full, and then kept on pouring. The professor watched the overflow until he could no longer restrain himself. "It is overfull. No more will go in!"

"Like this cup," Nan-in said, "you are full of your own opinions and speculations. How can I show you Zen unless you first empty your cup?"

We are thinking creatures, and like the professor in this story, in every moment we are like cups overflowing; carrying around with us any number of thoughts, opinions, and stories, all clamoring for our attention. In order to achieve inner peace, we must learn how to empty our cups and sit with silence and stillness in our minds.

One of the great gifts of the Buddhist tradition, hinted at in the story above, is the teaching that we exist beyond the tumble of thoughts that occupy our lives and, in fact, that the very notion of the "self," built on the foundation of the thinking mind, is actually a fiction. In Eastern tradition this is referred to as *anatta*, or "no-self."

We've already covered that you are not your body and you are not your emotions. Similarly, like Buddhism teaches and most schools of shamanism agree with, *you are not your mind*. This may be the most difficult concept we've covered so far to grasp, however, because our culture tells us all the time that we *are* our thoughts. But the reality is that your mind—like your emotions and body—is a material extension of your immaterial spirit. Right now, you're concentrating your attention on reading and simultaneously reflecting on the teachings here. But there are other voices in the back of your mind contemplating completely unrelated matters, like your grocery list. Those voices certainly aren't you, so who are they? They're your mind.

Your mind is like your breath—you have some moderate ability to control it, but otherwise it controls itself. You don't have to consciously breathe, as it happens automatically, though you can choose to breathe consciously when you want to. Likewise, you don't have to intentionally think—you can initiate thoughts intentionally, but otherwise, they just arise beyond your control. Your mind is another sensory field, but rather than sensing light or sound, the mind senses thoughts.

Though physical sensations are gateways to the present moment, thoughts are always *about* something, so they can only pull you out of the moment to reflect on that something. The mind reflects on experiences and then projects back narratives about them. These narratives color our perception and distort our view of what's happening.

But let's be clear. Logical, analytical, and critical thinking is not really the problem. The problem is allowing your analytical mind to dominate your perception of reality and unduly influence your behavior. Remember that we're addressing the challenge of determining and living your purpose. In this context, analytical thinking is useful in solving logistical problems in pursuing your purpose, but it can't help you determine what your purpose should be. *Life's existential challenges cannot be solved with logic.* Trouble only arises when we cannot disengage from logical thinking when it's no longer needed.

If the body is for acquiring physical power and the heart is for giving away emotional power, the mind is for *receiving knowledge*. You should use your mind to openly receive knowledge from all sources, expanding your thoughts and your worldview, and remaining flexible to changing with new information.

But most importantly, if the mind is for receiving knowledge, that means it is *not* for determining your direction. If you let the mind determine your life choices, you'll be relying purely on logic, which could lead to emptiness and boredom. Or worse, you may end up relying on illogical mental distortions while thinking you're being practical.

Our minds are constantly overstimulated, and because we've become accustomed to it, we have forgotten how to let the mind rest. It's important to balance the day's mental stimulation with intentional periods of quiet so that your mind can refresh itself.

Inviting Peace in the Mind with Meditation

We've already explored some exercises that can be powerful methods for cultivating peace in the mind, and that's because mindfulness and meditation practices are uniquely suited to this work. In fact, meditation is often one of the first practices that people think of when they consider ways to still their thoughts and cultivate mental peace.

There is something of a misunderstanding, however, that is common among beginning students of meditation that says that the goal of meditation is to achieve a mind empty of all thought. While a mind clear of *all* thoughts may be something that some practitioners eventually attain, meditation, especially in the beginning, is much more about the unattached observation of thoughts as they come and go in the mind. An apt metaphor for this is watching clouds pass over the peak of a mountain: the clouds are not permanent; they form, float, and disperse as air currents and temperatures change, but the mountain doesn't try to hold on to them. Thoughts inevitably arise because that is what the mind does—when we refuse to latch on to those thoughts, they will naturally move through and beyond us. What remains in the silent space beneath, ever-present, is peace.

Taking conscious time out of your day to sit in silence is akin to cleaning your house and setting the table in anticipation of a visit from a dear friend. Meditation in this way can be considered an invitation. To go deeper into finding peace in your heart's emotional center, consider maintaining a regular mindfulness or meditation practice. There are several meditation techniques to choose from, as well as a number of techniques throughout this book, so feel free to explore as many as you like in pursuit of the one that is the best fit for you. Many people have discovered that by setting out the welcome mat for inner peace in this way, on a regular basis, their ability to witness and release their thoughts, mental stories, and emotions increases enormously.

I also recommend doing breathwork. Working with the breath is an excellent way to still both the mind and the body simultaneously. I've outlined two practices below that can get you started. Either would be an excellent basis for a regular meditation practice.

Practice: Four-Point Breathing

The breath is connected to the mind, and the mind is connected to the breath. When the breath speeds up, the mind speeds up. When the breath slows down, the mind slows down. When the breath is short and shallow, you take in less oxygen (the power in the air). In response, your brain releases cortisol, the stress hormone, which agitates you even further. But when the breath is long and deep, you take in more oxygen, and your brain releases the pleasure hormones, deepening your calm. Finally, when the breath stops, the mind stops too.

To gain control of the mind, begin by controlling the breath. This is a great technique to use to settle your mind when it's particularly agitated.

As usual, sit comfortably, take a few deep breaths, and relax your body. Once you are settled, abide in your restful posture for a moment, just appreciating coming back to your center.

To practice four-point breathing, you'll follow these simple steps: First, take a deep inhale for four seconds. Hold it for four seconds. Fully exhale for four seconds. And hold the out-breath for four seconds.

Let's look at this practice a little closer. When you're ready, take a long, deep breath in through the nose for four counts. Deliberately expand the belly, inflate the chest, and lift the shoulders, sucking in as much air as possible until you are about to pop. Imagine the power in the air entering you as scintillating energy.

Hold your breath as you count to four again.

Exhale fully through an open mouth as you count to four. Deliberately contract the belly, deflate the chest, and drop the shoulders, blowing out as much air as possible until you are empty. You may feel the panicked urge to take a breath. Do your best to resist this urge and you'll notice the panic subside.

Hold your breath as you count to four again. You may not be able to fully exhale or hold the out-breath on your first try. Don't be disheartened. Just take that as a sign that you need to practice proper breathing.

When you feel ready, repeat the process, inhaling once more. You may notice your lungs reflexively opening wider for the next inhale. That's the diaphragmatic response we're training to inhale deeper and consume more energy.

Continue breathing in this manner for a few minutes. If at any point you get dizzy, light-headed, see stars, or your vision goes red, immediately stop the exercise and resume normal breathing.

After a few minutes of practice, you'll find that your mind has become fully absorbed in the breath. You'll also notice heat rising in the body. With practice, you'll even sense tingles of energy creeping up your arms and back.

Resume normal breathing and observe how you feel now compared to when you began. If you're new to breath-work, you may feel out of breath or exhausted, as if you just had an intense aerobic workout. That's because you did! The more you practice, the more you'll find the afterglow of the breathwork exercise is peacefully calm and spaciously clear.

Indulge in whatever calm and clarity you feel now. Become fascinated by any energy sensations the practice triggers. And simply notice how your natural breathing has become slower, deeper, and fuller.

As your breath gets stronger with practice, you can extend the four-count to five, six, and so on. Very gradually increase the length of each inhale, exhale, and pause between. Let the practice be just stimulating enough to captivate the mind, but gentle enough to relax.

Practice: Three-Point Breathing

Three-point breathing is great for when your mind is dull, drowsy, and depressed. It rouses the mind from inertia and gets it moving.

Once again, sit comfortably, take a few deep breaths, and relax the body. Get centered and repose there for a moment, appreciating the simple pleasure of coming to rest.

In this practice, you take two quick inhales followed by one long exhale.

When you're ready, take a quick, sharp inhale through the nose, like an aggressive sniff, while inflating the chest.

Take a second quick, sharp inhale through the nose, this time lifting the shoulders.

Finally, exhale fully through the mouth while sucking the belly in to flush air out of the lungs. When you're empty of breath, take another quick inhale through the nose and repeat the process.

Start slowly so that you can mindfully synchronize the breath with the body. Then gradually increase speed and you'll feel heat and tingling energy rising up the arms to the head.

Continue for up to one minute and then resume normal breathing. Your natural breath should now be faster, and your exhale should be stronger. The three-point breath trains the diaphragm to close and thereby enhance your power of exhalation.

Most of us do not breathe correctly without training. Unrefined, your breathing tends to be shallow. You inhale only to partial lung capacity and then interrupt the inhalation by exhaling too soon. Likewise, you exhale only enough to partially empty the lungs and then interrupt the exhalation by inhaling too soon.

Interrupted breathing not only causes you to receive less oxygen, but also to accumulate carbon dioxide in the lungs. In shamanic terms, you're receiving less power and accumulating stale, used, unwanted energy. The body thrives on the vital energy received through breathing. Interrupted breathing is one of the most common underlying causes for physical, emotional, and mental health problems.

The breathing exercises here will train you to stop interrupting your breath, enabling you to absorb more positive power with each inhale and release more negative energy with each exhale. As you strengthen your natural breathing and develop breath control, you'll easily be able to settle, energize, or pause your mind as needed.

Power in the Mind

When you bring the mind to rest, you learn whatever knowledge you need—often in a sudden, intuitive flash of insight. With a clear mind, you become fully present in the moment and know whatever you need to know. Then, your mental power is at your service, rather than distracting you. It's when you're mentally distracted that you have difficulty responding to challenging situations. The batter on the mound, the ballet dancer on the stage, the bomb squad technician—they all must maintain mental clarity to perform powerfully.

Imagine the mind is a lake. When the lake is still, you can see into its depths even as the surface reflects the sky above. Likewise, when the mind is still, you can see into the depths of your subconscious while reflecting the wisdom of your superconscious. But when you throw a pebble into the lake, it causes ripples that render the depths invisible and the surface no longer reflects the sky. Likewise, when you throw a thought into the mind, it causes agitation that renders the subconscious invisible and the superconscious inaccessible. We cannot force the lake to settle, but we can stop throwing pebbles into it and let it settle on its own.

Now imagine the mind is a walkie-talkie. You can broadcast yourself with a walkie-talkie, and you can receive broadcasts with your walkie-talkie, but you cannot do both at the same time. Likewise, when you're thinking, you're broadcasting. If you want to receive insight and wisdom from your superconscious, you need to stop broadcasting—stop thinking—and just listen. That is the essence of the being and not-doing practice: to stop and listen.

The being and not-doing practices in chapter 2 taught you the foundational methods to practice resting, and a regular meditation practice will give you a foundation from which to work. But if you've ever struggled to fall asleep because you had something on your mind, then you know how challenging it can be to cajole the mind into relaxing when it becomes attached to a story or thought. To move deeper into the work of the mind, we can build upon the earlier foundations by strengthening and refining our mental awareness.

You can't control the mind any more than you can control a puppy with boundless energy. But you can gently and repeatedly encourage the mind to rest. With gentle encouragement and practices like mindfulness, meditation, and breathwork, you can gradually train the mind to obey. The mind will continue to have its own will, but it will eventually defer to you rather than lead you around.

Practice: Stopping the World

Meditation and breathwork are enough to quell the mind most of the time, as they create conditions that encourage the mind to rest. But they do not directly train the mind.

The mind is always thinking about reality and telling stories about it. These stories color and distort your perception of the world to such a degree that you mistake the stories for reality. The mind goes on conjuring its own worlds all day and night. The trouble is that you live in this story world rather than the real moment-by-moment experience of reality. When you drop the story world, you become present, and the unconditioned fullness of each moment becomes available to you.

The story world depends on words, and your mind's internal dialogue provides an endless supply. The internal dialogue is a tether that anchors you in your story world. Even now, as you concentrate on reading these words, your mind's internal dialogue is likely running in the background of your awareness.

But you can break this tether and awake from the story world. By cutting off the mind's monologue, you interrupt the creation of your story world—and for a moment, you experience true reality in all its shining glory. This practice is called "Stopping the World" because it's a method for stopping the mind's world-making.

To stop the world and awake from your storytelling, you must stop the constant chatter of the mind. But you can't do it by force. Try to stop thinking now and see how impossible it is. Instead, the internal dialogue must be coaxed and cajoled like a puppy.

Set a timer for ten minutes. Sit comfortably with your back straight. Close your eyes. Take a deep breath in through the nose, and let it out through the mouth. Again, inhale through the nose, and exhale through the mouth. Take one more big breath in through the nose, sip in a little extra air, and hold the breath to a count of five. Exhale, fully emptying the lungs. Relax and breathe normally.

Practice centering to settle your energy and slowly disengage from outer distractions. Progressively draw your attention to your body, and then the breath. Once you're comfortably enjoying the sensations of breathing, then you can begin stopping the world.

All you must do is pay attention to your breath as it enters and leaves your body, as we did in the earlier practice. But this time, we're going to zoom in further on the breath either in the belly, the chest, or the nostrils. Choose the spot where you can sense the breath easily.

Really pay attention to the breath at your chosen spot. You're not looking for anything unusual, just the normal sensations of breathing. Become curious about the breath and examine it.

Set a gentle intention to keep your attention focused on the breath. You won't actually be able to keep your attention on the breath for very long, and that's okay. It's a gentle intention, not a goal.

As you're meditating, at some point you'll inevitably forget the breath and your mind will begin to wander (i.e., you'll start daydreaming, thinking, planning, etc.). As soon as you realize this, congratulate yourself for noticing. Take a moment to indulge in the satisfaction of having successfully noticed mind-wandering. And then gently guide your attention back to the breath and start again.

Every time you realize you are mind-wandering again, rejoice! Congratulate yourself for remembering rather than condemning yourself for forgetting. This step—congratulating the mind for remembering—is the essential step of the technique. This moment of congratulating yourself is a treat for the mind, so abide in the feeling of success for a few breaths. Then slowly return to the breath, reset your gentle intention to stay focused on it, and start again.

Each time you realize you've forgotten the breath, you'll experience a little aha moment. The game is hunting those moments of realization and celebrating whenever you remember to come back to the breath.

Think of it this way: Every time your attention wanders away from the breath and you draw it back, you're doing one rep of a mental exercise that's strengthening your attention muscle. The core cognitive skill we're developing here is attentional control.

Continue this cycle of focusing, forgetting, remembering, celebrating, and then focusing again. Repeat until the timer rings. If you get drowsy at any point, try three-point breathing to remain alert. If your body becomes restless, allow it to move however it wants, but do so in slow motion.

When the bell rings, take three more big breaths in through the nose, exhaling through the mouth. On the last inhale, hold the breath to a count of five before exhaling fully. Notice how your mind feels now compared to when you started. Has your internal dialogue calmed down or stopped? Notice without judgment, only curiosity. Then wiggle your fingers and toes, and gently blink your eyes open.

As you practice regularly, you'll notice that when your mind becomes absorbed in the breath, confabulation stops. The more you practice, the more easily you'll be able to access this mentally clear state.

Keep practicing these ten-minute sessions every day. Gradually, you'll notice the mind-wandering faster and faster. Then you'll notice that you're spending more time with the breath than mind-wandering. Eventually, you'll find that you're focused on the breath for the entire ten minutes with barely any mind-wandering.

Once you reach that point, extend your daily sessions to twelve minutes. Stay there for a few weeks, or until twelve minutes feels easy. At a certain point, when the timer rings, you'll think to yourself, "Ah, I wish I could stay here just a little longer." When you feel that thirst for more, then extend your session to fourteen minutes. In this manner, very gradually extend your sessions over time until you are comfortably practicing for twenty minutes to an hour.

The essential benefits of the practice emerge when you sit for twenty to forty-five minutes, and you'll discover a profound change in the way your mind behaves throughout your day. The deepest states of mental quiet and clarity occur when you sit for longer than forty-five minutes, but don't worry about getting there. Just enjoy the few minutes you're investing here and now.

Let this meditation be a daily refuge for you to disengage from the rigors of life. Some days the practice will feel effortless, and other days very effortful. Enjoy the satisfaction when it's easy and enjoy the challenge when it's hard. Don't worry about mastering the technique, because there's no such thing. Just patiently develop the skill of controlling your attention, one sit at a time.

The first time I successfully stopped my world, I didn't notice until after it started again. There was a momentary lapse in my stream of consciousness, as if someone had cut a few frames of the movie in my head. I only noticed the lapse in awareness after it happened, but I was fascinated by that tiny moment when my internal dialogue halted and my perceptual world collapsed. As soon as my mental dialogue stopped running, reality stopped being separate from me, and I became connected with everything.

Sound, sight, and sensation all collapsed into pure awareness without thought.

But just as quickly the world rushed back in, loud enough to jolt me out of my state. With practice, I found I could stop the world more and more easily and for longer durations. Initially, the moment of silence lasted only a microsecond. Then, little by little, it endured for longer stretches of time. This practice was tedious at first, but after that first taste of a silent mind, I was hooked and needed more.

Insight and Intuition

When you get a tarot reading and a stranger knows things about you they couldn't possibly know, it's an inspiring and magical experience. But that doesn't compare to being on the other side of the table, where you get to see readings working repeatedly for stranger after stranger. It truly is an inspiring and magical thing.

I've done thousands of tarot readings over the years, so I've felt this magic many times, and I still can't explain it. People often ask me how it works or what I'm doing exactly, and the truth is, I'm not doing anything.

During a reading, I'm not thinking about the questions people ask me. I'm not considering what advice I might give, or what I might do in that situation. I'm not recalling similar situations I've experienced. I'm not contemplating spiritual teachings. In fact, I'm not thinking at all.

I begin my workday with at least an hour of meditation where I bring my internal dialogue to rest. In this state of peace and presence, I sit with my clients and listen. When it's time to answer, I open my mouth and speak. But even then, I'm only allowing the words to come out of my mouth—I'm not consciously choosing them. Whatever I say in this state often ends up being what others need to hear. But I cannot take any credit for it. Spirit is the one watering you with knowledge; the reader is just a faucet.

But I do walk around all day doing my best to be present. In that state, even when I'm not working in my office, as I'm out and about living my life, I still find that my words and actions profoundly affect people in positive, transformative ways. The only magical thing I'm doing is getting out of my own way and allowing something greater to pull my strings.

What's even more fulfilling is that I know it's possible for others to unlock their intuition the same way—I've seen it happen. Just as I'm astonished that reading after reading works, I'm likewise amazed that class after class, total beginners receive profound insights after even just a few minutes of practice.

In a class several years ago, for example, two of my students, Jim and Beverly, shared an amazing psychic connection. In my classes, I first lead everyone through a meditation for quieting the mind, and then I tell the group to pair off and sit facing their partner. Each pair gazes at each other for a few minutes before closing their eyes and imagining their partner's face. They are then told to simply relax control and let their mind conjure images, ideas, or feelings without judgment or skepticism. Afterward, everyone takes turns sharing what they saw and discovering what resonates with their partner.

In that particular class, Jim and Beverly were both novices making their first attempt at exploring their psychic ability. When it was time to share what they had seen, Beverly insisted that her vision was nonsense and probably had no meaning for Jim. But I insisted she share what she saw anyway.

She said that all she saw was a butterfly fluttering around him. Suddenly, Jim's eyes welled with tears. An uncomfortable tension hung over the class for a few moments; students do often gain insights about their partners that touch on deeply sensitive subjects, and this can sometimes be awkward.

When he'd composed himself, Jim explained that his grandmother had raised him and that she loved butterflies. As she was dying, she promised that she would send a butterfly to him as a sign that she was still there. Sure enough, the morning after his grandmother passed, a butterfly appeared at his window in the dead of winter. Profoundly moved by this experience, he made it a habit of secretly drawing butterflies into his artwork. He never told anyone about the butterfly or what it meant to him. Yet after just a few minutes of practice, Beverly, a completely inexperienced stranger, was able to see Jim's secret butterfly.

The entire class was moved by Beverly's insight. Beverly learned to trust her intuition and stop second-guessing herself, and Jim received another sign that his grandmother's spirit was still with him and always would be. It was a powerful day!

Following the practices here will give you the awareness necessary to intentionally bring your mind to rest even amid the most stressful and overstimulating situations. With the mind at rest, you'll be completely present in each moment. Free of mental stories *about* what's happening, you'll be absorbed in what's *really* happening.

In this state of presence, you spontaneously know, say, and do whatever needs to be known, said, or done. That's really what it means to be psychic or intuitive: to be present enough to know and say what the moment requires, and nothing more.

Being spiritually aligned doesn't mean you're having psychic visions or communing with spirit entities all the time. It's simply quieting your internal dialogue and listening. In that state, you receive insight and wisdom that you otherwise can't hear.

If you can disengage from your body, heart, and mind as needed, you can connect to the underlying spirit that drives everything. And when you connect to that, you become it, and its power becomes yours. The cosmos, spirit,

God—whatever you want to call it—then acts through you and you become a conduit for the magical healing of others, the community, and nature. In this state, even as you're just out and about living your life, you'll find that your spontaneous words and actions profoundly affect people in positive, transformative ways. When you get out of your own way, you allow something greater to pull your strings and something magical can happen.

Now you understand why it's unwise to use your mind to determine your life path. Our choices are based on stories. They're useful when addressing how to walk your path, but they can't help you choose which path to walk.

So if you shouldn't let your body, heart, or mind determine your path, then what's left? Now we're ready to talk about the power of spirit.

Chapter Five

Peace and Power in the Spirit

If you are not your body nor emotions, and you are not your mind, this begs the question: who or what are you, then? Many shamanic schools teach that beneath the layers of your body, heart, and mind, at your most essential level, you are the *conscious energy* that emanates physical, emotional, and mental fields of experience. In modern-day language, the word we usually use for this is *spirit*. Thus the popular saying that "you are a spiritual being having a human experience."

Sometimes the truth of this is clear, but much of the time we become so absorbed in the physical, mental, and emotional fields that we forget our true spiritual nature. Even though we've spent several chapters digging into the details, it's so important that I'll say it one more time: you are not your body, heart, or mind; you are a spirit who *has* a body, heart, and mind.

We know now that when we possess inner peace, we express outer power, which is another way of saying we've attained spiritual awareness. And when we live with spiritual awareness, we spontaneously know, say, and do whatever is necessary, thus powerfully fulfilling our unique purpose in each moment.

Now, you may accept that living in the present moment is empowering, but you might disagree that simply living in the moment will magically give you the ability to do what each unique situation demands. And if your spirit were separate from everything and everyone else, you would be right. But your spirit is not and cannot be separate from everything and everyone else because everything and everyone is comprised of the same ultimate spiritual energy.

Saying that the fundamental energy of all things is spiritual just means that that energy is conscious or inherently alive. We can deduce that the energy is conscious because we are that energy and consciousness is our defining feature.

Your spirit—your consciousness—and the spirit of the entire cosmos and all the beings in it are one and the same thing. This idea sits at the heart of many different mystical traditions, but it's actually a very simple truth. Each of us is an expression of the same universal process that sparked the Big Bang and everything since. Here, that universal creative power is expressing itself as me, and there, it's expressing itself as you.

We can call this greater, transpersonal consciousness Great Spirit because it is the spirit, or consciousness, of everything. Other traditions may call it *chi, nagual, wakan, baraka* . . . it has countless names in many cultures and traditions, who interpret their perception of this universal force to mean that the cosmos is itself awake with consciousness. You can agree with that, or you can take it to mean that consciousness is an inherent quality of whatever the universal creative process is. Great Spirit is not an invisible deity in the sky to be worshipped but a term for the singularity of everything, the view from which the entire existent reality is a single point.

If Great Spirit is the bonfire, each of us is a candle lit from that fire. My flame appears to be mine, and your flame appears to be yours. But every flame came from the one great bonfire, so every flame is still just a piece of the greater flame. Even when all the candles are extinguished, the bonfire remains. And you can light an infinite number of candles from a single flame without the flame losing any of its power. Likewise, your spirit is a tiny spark of the Great Spirit. Put another way, you are Great Spirit temporarily pretending to be you.

I'll use myself as an example. In mundane awareness, "I" am Nabeel. I live, work, and play. But in spiritual awareness, I am Great Spirit living, working, and playing as Nabeel, and Nabeel is just something I'm aware of among other thoughts, feelings, and sensations. I am the universal energy that is everything, and I happen to be emitting as Nabeel right now. But Nabeel comes and goes even as I remain. Nabeel falls asleep and disappears, and while he's sleeping, I can pretend to be entirely different people altogether and yet still unchangeably me. Nabeel may get absorbed in the content of his experiences, but I am absorbed by experience itself.

In other words, Nabeel is the name for my ego, whereas Great Spirit is the name for who I really am. To say that you are Great Spirit just means recognizing that you are no different from the entire universal process of creation—whatever it may be—and that your ego is just who you're pretending to be.

When you drop your attachment to your ego identification, you instantly return to your natural state as an emanation of universal energy. As an emanation of universal energy, your power can and will flow exactly where the universal energy requires it. That's how just by maintaining spiritual awareness, you can know, say, and do whatever is needed—because you're not the one doing it anymore. You're letting the ultimate flow of universal power take over.

So spirit is what you are at your most essential core, but the spirit voice is easily drowned out by sensations, feelings, and thoughts. You block spiritual awareness when you're preoccupied with your mental stories and get sucked into the drama of your ego world. As you learn to bring the body, heart, and mind to rest, your underlying spirit shines through, and you hear its voice clearly. Your spiritual awareness intuitively guides you to your purpose.

When you're spiritually aware, you still experience the physical, emotional, and mental waves of life's ups and downs. You still experience pain, loss, and grief. But you're able to digest difficult experiences in their greater holistic context as part of a grand and mysterious universal process. When confronted with the fragility of life, you won't retreat in fear; you'll be astounded by how miraculous and precious life really is.

But most importantly, when you're spiritually aware, you can determine your path according to your spirit and stop being ruled by your body, heart, or mind. When anchored in the peace of your spirit, knowing arises spontaneously. Whatever choices you must make, you make confidently without analysis or soul-searching.

Cultivating Peace in the Spirit

All the previous practices in this book are intended to cultivate spiritual awareness since they help you rest in the present moment. Whenever you can abide in the present moment, undistorted by feelings, unperturbed by thoughts, your spiritual awareness shines through. But most of us still have a difficult time hearing our spirit voice and knowing what we're meant to do. The following practice will help enhance your sense of peace in the spirit and your overall self-awareness so that you can more clearly articulate your spirit voice and power.

Practice: Four-Point Check

The four-point check is a simple practice of articulating how you feel in your body, heart, mind, and spirit. It's often difficult for us to determine where our feelings are coming from, and it's even harder to tell which impulse is spirit and which is mind, body, or heart. By regularly articulating how your four powers are doing in each moment, you can develop clearer self-awareness.

You can also practice this exercise with others. Rather than saying, "Fine, thanks," when someone asks how you're doing, tell them how all four of you are feeling, and then invite them to share the same. This practice is also excellent for couples—regularly checking in with your partner on all levels will deepen your intimacy.

To perform the four-point check, simply ask yourself four questions:

1. How do I feel in my body?

2. How do I feel in my heart?

3. How do I feel in my mind?

4. How do I feel in my spirit?

Let's try this right now. Take a few minutes to notice your body. Does it feel comfortable or uncomfortable? Relaxed or tensed? Pleasurable or painful? Savor any comfort, relaxation, or pleasure you feel. If there's any discomfort, tension, or pain, then lovingly respond to your body's needs.

Next, does your heart feel happy or sad? Full or empty? Open or closed? Savor whatever happiness, fullness, or openness you feel right now. If there's sadness, emptiness, or the heart is closed, can you label the emotions you're experiencing? Can you release any unwanted emotional charge? Do you need to express what you've been feeling? Digest the emotion, express it, and then let it go.

Next, is your mind calm or agitated? Clear or confused? Concentrated or distracted? Savor whatever calm, clarity, or concentration you feel. If there's agitation, confusion, or distraction, disengage from work and stimulation to get centered.

Finally, how does your spirit feel? Is your spirit powerful or weak? Shining or dark? Connected or disconnected? Savor any power, light, or connection you feel. If there's weakness, darkness, and disconnection, become curious about why they're there and what they're telling you is wrong. Listen closely without thinking about it, and you'll intuitively know what's missing. The more you try to articulate how your spirit feels in comparison to your body, heart, and mind, the better you'll get at it.

From this place of awareness, you can then make clear choices about how to proceed: When your body is in pain, for example, you can address your physical needs by focusing on rest, exercise, or eating nourishing foods. When your heart is anxious or depressed, openly share your feelings rather than bottling them up. When your mind is agitated or stressed, disengage from reading the news or other overstimulating activities. These seem like small, common-sense activities, but we can't take these healthy and important balancing actions if we're not aware of needing to do so in the first place. You'll only know to make any of these adjustments if you practice checking in with yourself.

After doing this practice regularly, you'll experience moments when your body may be in pain, your heart may be hurt, your mind may be agitated, and yet somehow your spirit is still full, connected, and at peace. Even when pain, hurt, or agitation are present, you find your spirit can still shine. This claim may sound extraordinary, but you've probably already experienced it. If you have ever sacrificed something for someone else, then you satisfied your spirit's desire for harmony over your body-heart-mind's self-interest.

For example, imagine a devoted parent struggling to feed their child. The parent may be hungry too, but no matter how desperately their body craves food, their spirit cannot imagine eating until the child is fed. The parent will happily feed the child and go hungry themselves because their spirit is better satisfied that way. To eat while allowing their child to go hungry would break both the parent's and the child's spirit.

By consistently performing the four-point check, you'll enhance your self-awareness and ability to express yourself.

But most importantly, the more often you force yourself to articulate what's happening within you, the clearer you'll be able to distinguish between your spirit, mind, heart, and body. Eventually, this practice will give you full awareness of your changing moods in real time and the ability to correct yourself mindfully. Only with this crystal clear self-awareness can you genuinely trust that you're really following your spirit above all else.

Working with Forgiveness

It's common for those who are walking this path and doing this kind of work to eventually come up against personal power blockages where forgiveness is needed. The exercise above, for example, may reveal these areas; when focusing on the general state of the spirit, some people begin to clearly sense a lingering unrest there, as though something is unresolved. I encourage you to journal about those feelings and see if there are places in your consciousness where the practice of forgiveness might bring additional peace and clarity to your spirit. This may be a situation in your past, an individual with whom you've had a difficult relationship, or even yourself. In fact, forgiving yourself is often harder than forgiving others.

What is forgiveness? It's hard to pin down, but ultimately forgiveness is a gift you give yourself. Forgiveness blooms when resentment, vindictiveness, and lingering emotional pain are released for good—it's an experience, and many people report feeling physically lighter, brighter, and freer when it happens to them.

It's important to clarify here that you do not have to forgive anyone who hasn't asked for forgiveness. If someone is asking for your forgiveness, then they have acknowledged their mistake and how it's harmed you, and you have the opportunity at that point to work through the issue with them. But until someone asks for forgiveness, you have no obligation to extend it. Nevertheless, you may forgive them in your heart by acknowledging that they're only human. You can express your feelings of anger to them and let them respond. If they do not acknowledge your feelings or ask for forgiveness, then you can move on without extending it.

Likewise, you should never feel as though you are forcing forgiveness by trying to forgive someone before you are ready to do so. The inability to forgive a serious wrong is not a spiritual failure! It is merely something to be aware of within yourself—write it down in your journal and let it rest for the moment if necessary. You can always come back to it at another stage in your journey to reassess. The path of the happy warrior is not a race or a competition, and no one is judging you on your progress. Forgiveness will feel right when it is right. The work in this book will set the invitation and lay the foundation, and you will know when to move forward with the work of forgiveness for any given issue.

When the time is right and you are able to forgive, whether others or yourself, a profound healing occurs for everyone involved. Just like when any emotion is expressed, the opportunity for healing the emotion is available. There is astonishing power in honesty. While there is always a risk when we choose to dig deep and do this difficult inner work, that risk is also the opportunity for magic to happen.

Practice: Forgiving in the Heart

When you're ready to begin the process of forgiving someone in your heart—whether or not you're ready to extend it to them openly—then start by visualizing the person in your mind and allowing yourself to feel any emotional charge that arises. If the person caused you intense trauma, this first step may be difficult. To avoid retriggering the trauma, approach the practice in small doses. Spend just a few moments feeling the difficult emotion.

Then imagine the person who harmed you as a little baby. Imagine cradling them in your arms as they sleep. Feel the smallness of their body and how vulnerable they are. Imagine feeding them and rocking them and see how easy it would be to love them as a baby.

Then imagine the person as an old, dying person. Imagine cradling them in your arms as they pass away. Feel the frailty of their body and how emotional they are. Sense how they might be filled with fear or regret as their end draws near. As they breathe their last breath, imagine letting them go and wishing them peace and rest. Take a deep breath in and exhale through the mouth, sighing out your difficult emotions.

Next, imagine yourself as a baby. Imagine cradling yourself and showering yourself with hugs and kisses. Feel how innocent and precious you are. Spend as long as you like here genuinely loving yourself.

Then, imagine yourself as an old, dying person. Imagine all your loved ones gathered around you to say good-bye. Feel the grief, fear, and sorrow you might feel when your time comes. But then exult in how beautiful your ephemeral life is, how precious each person and moment has been. Let these emotions crescendo into peaceful acceptance. Imagine taking your last breath and exhale through the mouth, sighing out your difficult emotions and letting everything go.

Spend a quiet moment in this still, peaceful place. Complete the practice by imagining the person who harmed you once again. Do you still feel an emotional charge when you think about them? If so, then repeat the practice over the course of a few days or weeks, depending on how traumatic the event was. Once you can imagine them with no emotional charge, then you've forgiven them in your heart. If the day ever comes that they acknowledge how they hurt you and seek your forgiveness, you will be able to give it to them wholeheartedly. But even if that day never comes, you'll be ready to let the pain go and peacefully move on with your life, unencumbered by anger or resentment.

Manifesting Power in Spirit through Curiosity

Of course, no matter how present and spiritually aware you are, you'll still have to make hard choices. You'll face defining moments when you must decide which direction you'll go. What career path should you choose? Where should you live? Who should you love?

If you've been committed to living as a happy warrior in the small moments, you'll intuitively know what to choose in these big moments. This is the manifestation of spiritual power. But what should you do when you get stuck, confused, and lost in doubt about your life path and purpose?

Your body tells you to obey desire. Your heart tells you to obey emotion. Your mind tells you to obey logic. But spirit tells you to follow your *curiosity*.

Curiosity is the voice of your spirit. Often, your curiosity will want to explore areas that your body finds unpleasant, your heart finds painful, and your mind finds illogical. But if you give yourself permission to explore that curiosity, you'll find yourself walking a fulfilling path. You'll find that thread of curiosity leads you to ideas, teachers, and traditions that totally change your life. You could not have arrived at these experiences relying on desire, emotion, or logic. Only childlike curiosity will take you anywhere worth going.

Most of us suppress our spirit and call that being a grown-up. We think that ignoring our childlike impulses makes us an adult. We ridicule people who live boldly as childish, and we wear our seriousness as a badge of honor.

The truth is that following our childlike impulses does not mean following our desires so much as it means following our curiosity. So many of us have given up arts, crafts, and hobbies to "grow up," and then we find ourselves feeling empty and dissatisfied. Following our curiosity doesn't guarantee we will become successful artists, entrepreneurs, or philanthropists, but it does guarantee that no matter what happens to us, we'll feel full just from the pleasure of doing something we enjoy.

Curiosity eventually becomes expertise, which leads to opportunities and career paths. But let's be clear: Fulfilling your purpose and choosing a career are not the same thing. Your purpose is fulfilled whenever you are in the present moment, following your curiosity, and spontaneously acting according to your values. There are many careers that can satisfy aspects of your curiosity, but no one career will satisfy them all. That's because your curiosity is always changing, and your purpose changes with it.

Avoid the common mistake of searching through a list of careers and trying to predict which one you would be good at and enjoy. Don't bother trying to retrofit yourself into an existing career box. Instead, follow your curiosity until it becomes passion and expertise. Then, you'll be focused and purposeful, and you can seek out opportunities to expand your curiosity into a career of your own design.

Then, that career can lead you to a place to live, and you can start encountering people on your same wavelength.

Now more than ever, a career doesn't have to mean a single profession you do your whole life. Let your career include as many professions and passions as your curiosity demands, and allow your career to transform as you do.

Granted, curiosity alone won't necessarily get you on the right path. You also need to have self-awareness about what your unique powers are. For example, you may be curious about outer space, but physical challenges may prevent you from realistically becoming an astronaut. By checking your curiosity against your powers, you can steer yourself toward becoming an astronomer instead, a path that will satisfy your curiosity but also properly utilize your unique power.

You will also need to check your path against your values. Power utilized only in the service of curiosity may lead to disharmony. When you're guided by spirit, you don't just do what feels good or even what's best for you. Instead, you do what's right and necessary in that moment, and what's best for everyone. Spirit is concerned with harmony first and foremost, and to that end your spirit may call you to take actions for the benefit of others, or even actions that hurt your self-interest but are for the greater good.

The happy warrior relies on their values to determine the right action, rather than rigidly adhering to a strict moral code that's inflexible to the complexities of reality.

It's easy to say that fighting is always wrong. But when an attacker is hurting someone innocent and defenseless and you have the power to fight, is it right for you to refuse? As soon as you think you have your moral code defined, reality will throw you a curveball that upends your rote responses. In such moral dilemmas, only your values can guide you to the most meaningful choice.

For example, in Native American traditions, Coyote is a trickster commonly portrayed as breaking divine law in ways that help human beings, similar to Prometheus in Greek myth who steals fire from the gods in order to give it to humanity. In Hindu mythology, the god Krishna, a flute-playing romantic who never lies, famously uses cunning trickery to defeat villains and attain victory for the forces of good. And in English folklore, Robin Hood is a celebrated thief who steals from the corrupt and gives to the poor. All these characters are morally ambiguous. But since they act according to their highest values rather than a rigid moral code, they flexibly determine what's right in each moment. Since they're all driven by love and not a thirst for power, like their opponents, their actions positively create harmony.

To really be confident in your life path choices, you need to find where your curiosity, unique powers, and personal values align. Since your curiosities, powers, and values are always shifting, you need to continually check in. You can use the method below, for example, every time you need a reminder of what drives you, what you're capable of, and what really matters to you.

Practice: Soul Revival

In the past, it was easier for people to hear their spirit voice without the distractions of modern life. We modern folk are better served by writing down our articulations rather than just knowing them internally.

Soul revival involves determining what your values and your gifts are.

First, write down a list of your values. Have you ever thought about what you value? Love, wealth, justice, power, nature, family, success, loyalty, truth, fame, pleasure—any of these could be values. You don't really "choose" your values. You already have values. This practice is just about recognizing what they are.

So what do you value? Consider what is most important to you and write those things down. This list is not a summary of objects you desire but of what really matters to you. After listing everything you value, look over your list carefully and circle your top three. These values are your nonnegotiable truths. These values are the unspoken code you need to live by to be spiritually whole.

If you're honest about what your real values are, you may find that you're currently living in ways that contradict your values. This kind of dissonance over time can drain your spirit. For example, if you value honesty but lie, you'll betray your spirit. If you value justice but don't speak against injustice when you see it, you'll betray your spirit. If you value nature but work in an industry that you know harms nature, you'll betray your spirit. Correcting this misalignment is essential to unlocking your power, and you can start by setting gentle intentions to make gradual changes.

Next, write down a list of your gifts. Have you ever really stopped to consider what your gifts are? What are your natural talents? What are the skills you've developed? What are the qualities others admire in you?

Your gifts may be subtle—how you make people feel, how you articulate things, how you handle stress. Let this list run as long as you can make it. Keep adding to the list as you acquire new skills and realize other positive attributes about yourself. Your list of gifts will never stop growing. By seeing your gifts written out, you can better appreciate the power you already wield and then deploy that power more effectively.

Next, write down a list of your weaknesses. What could you be better at? Be honest, but don't be too hard on yourself. These weaknesses don't define you; they're simply a jumping-off point for your self-development work. Seeing them written out and named gives you power over them. Set gentle intentions to work on refining the skills you lack.

Finally, write down a list of your curiosities. Which subjects have always fascinated you? Art, history, science, spirituality, magic, engineering, linguistics? There's no end to the possibilities. It's certainly possible for any of us to go on forever with a list like this (there is so much to learn, see, and do in this world), but try to focus your list on the curiosities that you keep returning to throughout different life stages. And it's okay if you can't identify any repetitive curiosity like that—just do your best.

By the time you finish this exercise, your soul should feel revived. Armed with a list of your values, gifts, weaknesses, and curiosities, you can make decisions that honor your values, utilize your gifts, strengthen your weaknesses, and explore your curiosities. This all adds up to your spirit being empowered by finally being seen, heard, and recognized.

Continually return to these lists to remind yourself what truly matters to you, how powerful you genuinely are, what you humbly need to work on, and what you're fiercely passionate about. Over time, your values, gifts, weaknesses, and curiosities will change as you gain new experiences, learn new lessons, acquire new skills, and discover new mysteries. Be sure to check in periodically and revise the list as you go.

When you're lost trying to determine your path, review your values, strengths, and curiosities to discover where they align. Directions that spark your curiosity, use your strengths, and honor your values will always be fulfilling.

In my own case, the thread of my curiosity led me to mystics, yogis, and shamans who opened doors to new worlds for me. Over time, my friends referred me to others, and a fulfilling, thriving career grew up around me. I did not have to *become* a healer. Loving and caring for others, holding space for people's suffering, and finding my own way out of my darkness made me a healer. Therefore I can say with confidence that your own path, born out of the realization of true inner peace within and the manifestation of your personal outer power, can grow up organically around you too. It is already all there.

Your spiritual purpose is not a predestined future objective to be achieved someday and somewhere out there. Your purpose must be lived and fulfilled *right here and now* without further delay. With a clear sense of your values, gifts, and interests, you can trust that whichever direction you go will be the best one.

Moving Forward with Peace, Power, and Purpose

Living in purpose is something we do whenever we cultivate inner peace and outer power in our bodies, hearts, minds, and spirits. You've done a lot of great work to get to this point, including articulating your values and your gifts. Along with that work, you've no doubt begun to realize that you have dreams and desires that naturally flow out of those values and gifts, and you may be wondering how best to use what you've discovered to achieve those dreams. So let's move even deeper to uncover how this new way of being can be applied to practical challenges and to creating a life of authenticity and joy. We'll explore two critical and complementary ways of doing this: the Way of the Gardener and the Way of the Hunter. Together, these two ways of approaching your dreams offer a holistic plan to achieving them in this life.

Let's begin with the Way of the Gardener.

Chapter Six

The Way of the Gardener

Common wisdom tells us that if we want to make our dreams come true, we must pursue them with single-minded and unrelenting focus. But if you do chase your dreams with this kind of narrow obsession, it's possible that your body will be neglected, your heart will be drained, and your mind will be fried in the process. This kind of imbalance could cost you your health, and it could do harm to your relationships too. When all else falls to the wayside in pursuit of a goal, meeting it doesn't guarantee that you will be any happier. In fact, you may even feel worse because you don't understand why attaining your goal didn't fill your emptiness.

I know this firsthand because I spent much of my life chasing dreams while ignoring what was in front of me. Obsessed with succeeding at all costs, I narrowed my entire identity around my obsession and stunted myself. I only snapped out of that mentality when I finally gave myself permission to explore my curiosity wherever it might lead.

Still, even as my curiosity slowly developed into expertise, I knew that developing my personal power wasn't enough. I had to find a way to materially thrive in the world—spiritual practice alone wasn't going to accomplish that. If I were going to enjoy prosperity and abundance, I had to create it myself. But first, I needed to figure out what success really means.

To put it simply, success is a garden, not a goal. The markers of success (wealth, political power, authority, etc.) may be achieved, but often they have little to do with actually making us truly happy. Material condition is not what determines success.

The problem with chasing success as a goal is that it delays happiness until the perceived finish line. And of course, the truth is that there is no finish line at all. Every successful client I've ever worked with has felt deep down that they haven't really "arrived." Every goal they accomplish reveals another goal further out to agitate about; there is no relief. When you're always working to advance, acting out of anxiety while calling it dedication, and perpetually hoping for some future win, you're unable to use your power in any meaningful way.

So here's the key: You won't be content when you achieve your goals—*you will achieve your goals when you are content.* By being and not-doing and balancing inner peace and outer power in your body, mind, heart, and spirit, you will experience a consistent sense of contentment. In that state, you effortlessly and joyfully do what needs to be done to move your life forward. I promise you that everything you have ever accomplished came from you feeling good first. While you felt good, you said, did, and created exactly what was needed.

Don't misunderstand me—it's good to have goals. But the trick is to do your work because it brings you joy here and now instead of putting joy on hold while you push toward some far distant finish line that may or may not actually exist. Joy is a choice in each moment, and the more you practice, the easier it gets. The more joyful you are, the more outgoing, creative, and inspiring you become.

The best metaphor and archetype I know of for engaging this joyful sense of abundance is that of the Gardener.

The Gardener

Imagine a gardener who spends all her time in her garden. She plants many seeds. She nurtures them with water, soil, and sunshine. She prunes the plants to keep them healthy. And eventually, her plants flower and bear fruit. Then she takes that fruit to the market and sells it, transforming it into wealth.

But the gardener does not spend all her time gardening for that one day at the market. If the wealth were what made her happy, she could have found easier, better ways to make more money. Instead, she chooses to spend her days gardening because *she loves to garden.* The act of gardening itself is what brings her joy. The fruit of her labor is a bonus, not her purpose. In fact, the purpose of selling in the market at all is not to make money but to fund another cycle of gardening!

You have creative ideas. These are your seeds. You probably agonize over which seeds to plant, but the gardener teaches us to plant *all* our creative seeds. That means when you have an idea, don't judge it as good or bad, since you're not able to predict how the vision may play out in real life. Instead, plant the seed by capturing the idea (write it down, record it), and then ask yourself, what is the first step in pursuing this idea? If that first step is something you can do, then do it. Your seed is planted! If the first step of your idea is not doable, shelve that idea for now, knowing that you can come back to it later to see if the ground is ready for that seed then.

Not sure if you should apply for a practical job or a dream job? Apply for both and see what comes back. Not sure which story you should write? Start both and see what happens. Not sure where to move? Look for jobs and apartments in both cities and see what shakes out. Stop worrying about determining the "best" trail up the mountain, and just start climbing! Throw spaghetti at the wall and see where it sticks!

The point is, you never know which ideas will connect and which won't. You're not able to assess that. Instead, you can only try throwing seeds into the soil and see what comes back to you. Cast a wide net and you'll catch some big fish.

Once the seeds are planted, the gardener nurtures them. She doesn't water just one seed but distributes her water evenly. When one plant sprouts ahead of the others, then she'll know to direct more water to that plant.

Let's say you're an artist or an entrepreneur and you've got many ideas for potential projects and businesses. Now that you're planting seeds, you know to start every creative project and get the ball rolling on every business idea. Whatever the first step on each of those paths is, take it. Initially, distribute your attention evenly among your various seeds.

Allow your curiosity to flit from interest to interest. Work on one idea until your curiosity is exhausted, and then shift to another, and so on, making your way around your garden, watering every seed a little bit. Don't force yourself to work on a project because you feel you "should." If your curiosity wants to switch gears, let it. Develop projects that satisfy your creative, professional, and philanthropic curiosities. Set aside time each day to play in your garden and during that time, let your curiosity jump from project to project as it wants.

In this manner, you'll enjoy every day because you'll get to play in your garden. But at the end of the week, month, or year, you'll look up from your play to find you've created a portfolio of work, launched a business, or made a meaningful difference. You don't have to box yourself in as a "creative" or a "professional." Allow your spirit to expand however it likes.

As a particularly relevant example, I first began writing this book a decade ago! At the time, I had no reason to write a book, yet my curiosity compelled me to do it anyway. All the while, my mind warned me that I was wasting my time and urged me to do something more productive. But I resisted the temptation to indulge my anxiety and wrote my ideas down anyway. Over the years, I'd open this book up again from time to time and add a little something. Years later, I was asked if I had any spiritual writing to share, and I suddenly realized why I had been writing that whole time. I never forced myself to come up with, write, and finish a book all in one fell swoop. In fact, I didn't even force myself to focus on just this project.

At one point, one plant might start growing faster than the others, and therefore require more attention. Likewise, as you're nurturing your various seeds, one project catches fire and picks up momentum ahead of the others. When that happens, you can then give yourself permission to divert your full attention to that project.

If you're working on three different business plans but investors get excited about one, that's the one to put your energy behind. If you're writing three different novels but a sudden flash of inspiration reveals the ending to one, then that's the one to focus on. Your other ideas can wait in your garden until you have the bandwidth to revisit them. When you do, you'll see those ideas with a fresh perspective, which prompts new curiosity.

Be disciplined only in the sense that you make time for play in your garden every day—or as often as your schedule allows. When playtime comes around, remember to really play. When you let your curiosity lead you, you nurture your projects rather than force them. Forcing yourself to create or perform is like yelling at your flowers to grow faster. Relax, and give yourself space and time to see what unfolds.

Finally, be sure that you're planting seeds that you're genuinely curious about. Many people want to be musicians but don't enjoy practicing an instrument. Many people want to be successful businesspeople but don't enjoy wheeling and dealing. Many people want to be published authors but don't enjoy writing. Many people are studying to become doctors, lawyers, and engineers, but they don't enjoy the work. It should be obvious that behaving in this way won't bring joy in the moment, and it won't bring you joy in the future either.

Remember, joy comes from the work itself and not the end result. The fruit of your work is not the reward. The fruit is what allows you to keep doing work that is itself rewarding.

Seed Collecting

The Way of the Gardener is a subtle shift in attitude with profound effects. By planting all your creative seeds, you avoid the pressure of having to pick just one impulse and can honor all of your interests and see where they lead. By nurturing all your creative projects and letting them grow at their own pace, you enjoy working on the projects themselves without waiting anxiously for the results to come back. By letting the growth of our projects determine where we should focus our energy, we avoid getting in the way of progress.

The more you play in your garden, the more it will flourish, and the fuller and more abundant your life becomes. Houses, books, and businesses are not built in a day. They are built brick by brick, letter by letter, step by step. It's the daily practice of adding a little more energy here, a little more energy there, that gradually develops lasting results.

Of course, you may come across times when you feel like you don't have any seeds to plant. That's where keeping a running list of ideas comes in. Gardeners, especially those who grow heirloom varieties, save seeds from previous plants to sow in the future. And even those who don't save seeds might have a collection of purchased seeds in their root cellar. (A friend of mine keeps seeds in the crisper drawers of an old fridge out in the garage.) These seeds are little pockets of potential each waiting for their moment. Likewise, you can create a seed bank of ideas for the future—and just as gardeners may dream of their spring garden and make plans for each seasonal task, you can break down your ideas into smaller tasks that lead to abundant green beds.

Practice: Circling Seeds

Make a list of everything you want to create. Do you want to write a book, make a painting, or start a business? Write down everything you feel called to make, no matter how silly, fantastical, or impractical it might seem. These are the creative seeds you're going to plant. Don't judge or rule out any option, just write every impulse down. You can revisit this list periodically to remind yourself what you wanted to create, and you can update it as your interests change.

Once you have a list of seeds, ask yourself, what is the first step to cultivating this seed? If you want to write a book, maybe the first step is planning and outlining. If you want to paint, maybe the first step is acquiring the tools or signing up for a class. If you want to start a business, maybe the first step is writing a business plan. Go through every seed on the list and write down the first step for each one.

Now ask yourself, are any of the first steps doable? If the first step is beyond your reach, then that's not doable. Leave it on the list for now, but don't bother investing much energy in it. Maybe later that first step will become doable, and then you can revive this seed. Until then, table that seed and move on to the next.

If the first step of an idea is doable, then ask yourself, would you *enjoy* doing it? If you want to write a book, would you enjoy being alone and writing for hours? If you want to paint, would you enjoy working with the paint and learning the techniques? If you want to start a business, would you enjoy working with numbers, managing people, and assuming leadership and responsibility roles? If the answer is no, then table that seed. Maybe later you'll find that activity does become enjoyable, and then you can revive that seed. Otherwise, move on to the next.

If the first steps are both doable and sound like fun to you, then those are the seeds you should water, which means taking that first step. Take the first steps on all your viable seeds. Once you've taken all the first steps of all the viable seeds, then circle back to the first one.

Now ask yourself, what is the next step on this project? Do not look further than a single step. After you've finished step one, this next step becomes step one. Determine next steps for all the seeds you've moved forward with.

Again, ask yourself if the next steps on these projects are doable. If so, ask yourself if you would enjoy the work of that step. If the next step is doable and sounds fun, then get to work on it.

Continue in this manner, gradually watering each of your seeds in turn, until one seed catches fire.

Eventually, one project will gain momentum and advance ahead of the others. When that happens, then you'll know where to focus your attention. Go hard on that project and see where it takes you. And then repeat this process all over again.

When you move in circles this way, there is no finish line. There is no final step. There is only ever one step: the step you're on. No matter how far your project goes, you can always come back and think of a new step to take it further. The fun never ends!

Cultivating Joy

The Way of the Gardener shows us the correct way to cultivate joy, creativity, and prosperity. When you become a gardener, you don't overanalyze your ideas; you just try them out. You don't stress about which interest to focus on; you just give yourself permission to let your curiosity flit between all of them. You won't need to predict which project will be the most viable, because whichever one catches momentum will reveal itself as needing more of your attention.

The gardener saves us from the sabotaging behaviors of overanalyzing, indecision, and projecting into the future. Maybe you're ignoring brilliant ideas that could change your life because you can't imagine how they could ever be realized. Stop trying to imagine it! Give attention to even your silliest, wildest ideas and impulses. Ask what the first step would be to pursue those ideas, and then take that step. See what happens. An idea you would have written off as impractical, illogical, or stupid may turn out to change your life or the world.

When you're gardening, you embrace the cyclical nature of time. You repeat the same actions in the same order, over and over again, year after year. You take joy from the action itself and do not expect to reach the end of the line. Some harvests are better than others; some years are better than others. But you know that by putting in the time consistently you have a chance of having a good year. By circling your interests in this way, growth generates and abundance inevitably blooms.

A Life of Abundance

Since applying the gardener's approach to my creative projects, I've entered the most prolific period of my life. I've written more, composed more music, and launched many more business projects than in all the years I obsessively chased success. Now, I honor every idea by capturing it, nurturing it, and letting it develop into whatever it will. Ideas that I would have dismissed before now turn out to yield the most exciting results. Without judging my ideas, I've discovered how to let them blossom in their own time.

As I spiraled through all the seeds I had sowed, I slowly expanded my garden outward until my seeds bore fruit and were able to feed me. Though it required a lot of hard work, I practiced enjoying the moments—the conversations I got to have, the people I got to meet—rather than joy-lessly charging toward an imaginary goal. When I realized that joy was not dependent on abundance, I was able to churn my joy into abundance. Ultimately, success is not the money or the possessions, it's the privilege of being able to do what we enjoy. Only by consistently doing what we enjoy can we ever hope to attain a fulfilling life.

Now you know the secret to manifesting any long-term dream. Through a combination of following your curiosity and cycling through all your interests/projects, you find joy in simply getting to play, and then success organically develops around you. Everyone knows that major accomplishments are attained one step at a time. The spiritual secret is anchoring your joy in the stepping rather than the accomplishing.

But what do you do when you're not trying to create something, but catch it? Some things in life aren't grown, they're seized. For example, you can create a work of art, but you still need to "hook" a buyer. You can grow a social community, but you may need to "catch" a lover. You can practice your instrument, but you still need to nail the audition.

The Way of the Gardener is only one half of the coin. When it's time to reach out and grab a chance that might slip away, you need to know the Way of the Hunter.

Chapter Seven

The Way of the Hunter

Hunting and gathering were essential skills for survival in prehistoric times. The Way of the Gardener is about gathering power and developing it into abundance and prosperity. The Way of the Hunter is about asserting that power to face your opponents and obstacles. If gardening is for creating your dreams, hunting is for capturing your desires.

While gardening is about savoring the activity without waiting for the result, hunting is inherently result-oriented. When hunting, the goal is clear, and the only possible outcomes are victory or defeat, whereas cultivating the garden of your life is more open-ended, with infinite possible outcomes. When you're creating, you need to approach the process of creation with the attitude of the gardener. But when you're trying to catch something before it's gone, you need to be a hunter instead.

The hunter develops five essential skills to catch her prey: stillness, secrecy, swiftness, strength, and surrender. Do you want a better job? Do you want to find love? Do you want to win a legal case? Whatever the goal is, you need to know how to hunt to properly attain it without exhausting yourself. Attaining our long-term goals requires patience, determination, and tenacity. But in a world where everyone is competing for success, love, and power, how do we navigate the trials of competition?

As a gardener, we cultivate the discipline to create step by step, piece by piece, without getting caught up in our own thinking. As a hunter, we use that same discipline to push through any of life's challenges.

The goal you choose should be determined by your spirit. Your curiosity, values, and awareness of your own body, heart, and mind guide you to the best determinations. Once you are determined and ready to act, then it's time to apply the Way of the Hunter.

Many people come to me when they're in a rut and desperate to turn their life around. One of my clients, Jane, was at such a crossroads. In her thirties, she was single, stuck in a career she hated, and consistently disrespected by family, friends, and employers. She'd lost hope of ever being happy, let alone finding love or a fulfilling career. She'd been burned by too many bad relationships, abused at too many miserable jobs, and neglected by her family one too many times. Her spirit was broken, and she'd lost all her power.

Having been let down so often, Jane was racked with fear and anxiety. Sadly, she was too terrified to dream about what she wanted out of life. When we sat down together, my first task was figuring out exactly what she wanted and what was really stopping her. We began with the first of the five essential skills: stillness.

Stillness

Jane was too scared to admit that she didn't want to be a nurse anymore and too embarrassed to admit that she wanted to pursue alternative healing instead. After all, nursing paid good money, and everyone would think she was crazy if she walked away from health care to chase some spiritual fantasy. To make matters worse, her family rejected all spirituality and she felt they would never understand what she wanted to do.

First, Jane had to cultivate stillness. For her, that meant never taking the bait when provoked. Rather than getting sucked into conflicts, Jane practiced keeping her emotional equilibrium by not engaging—not defending herself or arguing, but simply removing herself from uncomfortable situations while focusing on her own goals, undistracted.

Stillness is not just the physical, mental, and emotional calm we cultivate in our not-doing practice. In the context of hunting, stillness means *waiting without impatience*. The stillness you develop by not-doing can then be used actively when you need to wait for the story to move forward. In our eagerness to win the fight, we rush into action haphazardly and without mindfulness. A good hunter's actions are deliberate, calculated, and premeditated. The hunter will wait until an opportunity arises.

Some days, there is nothing to be done. If you're in a legal battle, you may be waiting for the other party to make a move. If you're job hunting, you may be waiting to hear back from a potential employer. If you're hunting for love, you may be waiting for a call. If you are impatient and agitated, you're not experiencing the full reality in each moment, which is the only place you'll ever find what you're hunting. When you're a hunter, you have no aversion to waiting, as you take it as an opportunity to rest rather than agitate about a lack of momentum.

This is active patience rather than passive. Passive patience is waiting for something to happen *to* you or *for* you. Active patience is calmly observing until you notice an opportunity. In a state of patiently waiting, you're not analyzing the situation, you're not reflecting on past mistakes, you're not projecting possible future outcomes. You're still, at rest, and keenly observing, watching, and listening for that right moment to act.

Practice: Perfect Stillness

Stillness is the core skill that everything else is built upon. The more you refine your ability to become totally still, the more easily you can maintain secrecy, act swiftly, be strong, and genuinely surrender. But it takes training to become still in stressful conditions.

In this exercise, you'll practice sitting perfectly still. While it may be challenging at first, I'll show you how to gently cultivate this crucial ability. Start a timer for ten minutes.

Sit comfortably, take a few deep breaths, and relax your body. Get centered. Draw attention into your body. Inhale deeply as you tense all your muscles, clench your fists, scrunch your face, etc. Hold the tension for about three seconds or until you're shaking. Then exhale, fully relaxing and letting the body go limp.

Notice the stream of sensations running from head to toe. Delight in any pleasure you feel in the body. Just as in the Stopping the World meditation, focus your attention on the breath at the belly, chest, or nose. When you forget the breath, congratulate yourself for remembering and gently return to it.

Your goal for the remainder of the session is to sit perfectly still. Of course, you won't be able to do that yet, and that's okay. When you have the urge to move, do your best to resist it. Take a deep breath and relax instead. You may find the urge to move dissipates. If the urge to move remains, then give yourself permission to move however you like, but *move in slow motion*. As you move in slow motion, curiously observe the sensations of the movement. When the movement is complete, return to stillness with another deep breath.

You may not only feel the urge to move, but also a variety of irritating sensations like tickles in the throat or itchiness. When an itch arises, resist the urge to scratch it. Take a deep breath instead, wait, and see if it dissipates. If the urge remains, bring all your attention to it and curiously examine the sensation of the itch. What is it, exactly? Is there really something on your skin, or is it just your nervous system misfiring?

You may be surprised to find that examining these sensations often causes them to dissipate. If they persist, then give yourself permission to move, but once again, move in slow motion. Continue in this manner until the timer rings.

Afterward, estimate how many times you moved. Note the number without judgment. If you moved ten times today, then next time aim to move only ten times. When moving only ten times becomes easy, then aim to move only nine times. Gradually, over many sessions, you'll find that you're able to sit for the entire session without any movement. Once you can sit for the entire ten minutes without moving, extend your session to twelve minutes, and so on.

When you start resting in this kind of relaxed stillness, you'll notice pleasant sensations of energy circulating through your body. You'll also find your mind becoming completely absorbed in the moment. With practice, you'll be able to experience the body as a rich field of circulating energy whenever you like, even when you're not meditating.

Secrecy

The next skill of hunting is secrecy. Hunters must move silently to approach their unsuspecting prey. Likewise, when you're pursuing your goals, secrecy is an important ally.

Secrecy is necessary for any real magic to happen. A seed only grows in the darkness of the soil; a child only grows in the darkness of the womb. To look in at the process of growth is to disturb it. So, whatever you're pursuing, be discerning in how much of your intent you reveal. Don't tell people you want to start a business—make a business plan. Don't tell people you hope to write a book—start outlining it. Don't tell everyone your plans—rather, let them find out naturally when you succeed.

When you're trying to manifest something and you share that intent with others, their expectations and assumptions will hamper your manifesting. Remember that reality is cocreated by you, spirit, and every other free being. If you overshare your every move, other people's expectations of your plan may affect its ability to be realized. The more you keep your intent secret, the more power you have in any given situation, and the more opportunities you'll discover on the hunt.

Of course, secrecy may not be relevant in all situations and circumstances. But when you're facing genuine adversaries, secrecy is essential to victory. You may already know what it's like to have your own statements come back to bite you. Words can definitely dismantle plans. A stray comment made in a moment of anger or frustration can lead to a string of negative consequences. But if you walk as a hunter, if you use secrecy as your ally, then you can ensure that your own words do not derail your mission.

We can sometimes sabotage ourselves by telling too many people about our dreams and ambitions. It only takes one dismissive eye roll from a skeptical friend to knock you off-balance. So be clear-eyed enough in your purpose to not need others to validate you along the way. Don't tell people who you are or who you want to be. Show them with your actions.

Don't misunderstand: secrecy is *not* about hiding malicious intent or scheming. Secrecy is simply about preserving the sanctity of your vision and not allowing other people (or social media, or even your own doubts) to pollute it before you can realize it. Secrecy is a powerful weapon when wielded wisely.

My client Jane had struggled with secrecy in the past. She had a history of sharing every up and down with everyone in her life. She had announced her pregnancy only to suffer a miscarriage. She had announced a new job offer before it was official, only to have it rescinded. This time, she practiced keeping her plans to herself. She set about taking courses in alternative healing and quietly gaining knowledge and credentials all without ever telling anyone. The hunt was on!

Swiftness

Stillness and secrecy, while powerful, are ultimately useless if they aren't paired with *swiftness*. Being swift means seizing an opportunity the moment it appears without hesitation.

Imagine a wolf waiting all day for the right moment. As soon as she sees her chance, she strikes without hesitation or deliberation. You can be actively patient all day, but if you lack the swiftness to seize opportunities in the moment, then your patience is fruitless.

Say you're hunting for a job and you meet a powerful person who could open doors for you. You've been waiting for this opportunity, but what do you do? You hesitate, you get nervous, you get scared. Then your chance is gone as quickly as it came, never to return. And you have only yourself to blame.

Time after time, when opportunity arises, we choke. That's because we lack swiftness. We cannot possibly be swift if our energies are out of balance. Remember that peace and presence are what give us power. Being swift does not mean intensely going, going, going all the time; you must know when the time is right through discernment, which comes naturally when you cultivate inner peace and presence. If you can truly be still and present, then you will automatically react swiftly and appropriately when the situation demands.

One key way to know when that moment has arrived is when you feel a thrill of fear. The risk and intimidation inherent in seeing your goal materialize right in front of you can often blaze through your nerves and set your heart beating faster—a typical fear response. This is the signal that you need to act *now*. Let this fear of the unknown be a signal that you should reach out and grab that goal. That's the only practice here: recognizing when an opportunity scares you and knowing that that's the moment to strike.

Jane's biggest challenge was developing swiftness. She'd let so many opportunities slip through her fingers because she had hesitated to act swiftly. Eventually, she learned to see that when something exciting scared her, it was a sign that she should barrel forward to see what would happen. Using this technique, Jane pushed past her fears. Suddenly, she was approaching people more confidently, unafraid to chat up a cute stranger or network with a potential contact. She started saying yes to invitations if she got even the slightest inkling that something good might come of it. Whenever a chance presented itself, she learned to take it and enjoy the ride. The more she acted swiftly, the easier it got, and the more fun.

When you lack swiftness, you end up saddled with regrets. But it's better to make mistakes and regret them than to regret missing chances. If you miss a chance, you'll never know what could have been, and that possibility will always haunt you.

Many if not most of our mistakes transmute into new strength. So in the end, even if you make mistakes, you won't regret them as much. The only lesson you'll learn from a missed chance is that you should have been swifter. So develop the skill of swiftness now, before it's too late!

Strength

Sometimes, even when you're swift and strike without hesitation, you miss. You'll meet defeat sooner or later. Failure happens. It's inevitable.

I'm not going to tell you that everything happens for a reason. You have free will, but so does everyone else. That means reality is a free-for-all where anything goes. Nothing is promised. You'll swing and miss. You'll try and fail. You will, many times throughout your life, taste the humiliating sting of defeat.

That means you must develop the skill of strength. Strength in this context does not mean brute force, but rather emotional endurance. Weakness in this case means falling into self-pity at the slightest sign of discomfort or imperfection. The hunter, however, expects neither comfort nor perfection. Instead of wallowing after a setback, the hunter musters their strength to keep going, to learn from defeat and try again.

Most of the people in Jane's life didn't support the direction she was choosing, so she had to find the strength to carry on despite opposition. Demands at her job intensified even as she was finally starting to build her alternative healing business. Her family became increasingly aggressive as her newfound confidence rattled them. They verbally attacked her to undermine her self-esteem. She was tempted to listen to their abusive criticism, but she endured. She avoided pitying herself when she saw other people in happy relationships, fulfilling careers, and peaceful families. She maintained her strength and forged ahead.

No one is promised success, partnership, and happiness. If you continually fall into self-pity whenever life gets tough, you will never catch your prey. In fact, you're banishing your power and adopting powerlessness and self-absorption as your new identity whenever you wallow.

We all suffer. We all experience defeat and hardship. Self-pity can only arise if you hold the belief that somehow you are supposed to be immune from suffering, defeat, and hardship. Self-pity can only arise if you thought you were special. The hunter does not delude herself in this way.

When a wolf strikes and misses her prey, she does not wallow in self-pity. She does not complain that her lot in life is too difficult. She has the strength to know that life is difficult and she must regroup and try again.

Surrender

Becoming absorbed in self-pity keeps you trapped in the past. To move forward in the face of defeat, the hunter *surrenders*. Surrender in this case doesn't mean giving up—it means accepting things as they are. The hunter knows that it's a mistake to take life too seriously and that relaxation and laughter are healthier responses to failure, so she surrenders to the way things are with ease and vows to try again. When you surrender, you stop pretending you're in control of the outcome and accept that life has its own flow.

The wolf surrenders herself to the wild. The stakes are life and death, and she does not expect anything else. She accepts the reality she can't change and adapts to it. Surrendering also means listening to reality when it's telling you to change course. When you keep hitting a brick wall in chasing your goals, surrendering might mean letting go of your goal altogether and seeing where reality leads you.

Once she was venturing down an exciting life path, Jane was finally able to surrender. She slowly accepted her family's limitations and found ways to coexist with them while firmly asserting her boundaries. She accepted setbacks and tried not to take the hunt too seriously. She laughed in the face of disappointment and kept going. But she also learned from those disappointments and made adaptations as necessary.

Putting It Together

Once we've surrendered, we then return to stillness as we resume waiting for the next opportunity. In this manner, we move through these five modes repeatedly until our goal is attained or a new path has opened.

First, wait in stillness, patiently watching for an opportunity. Second, shroud your intent in secrecy to keep your purpose clear and unsullied. Third, strike swiftly the moment opportunity arises without deliberation or hesitation. Fourth, rely on your strength to persevere. Fifth, surrender in the face of defeat, laugh off the game, and accept that reality may have something else in mind for you. And finally, circle back to stillness and begin the cycle again.

Ask yourself, have you been acting like a hunter?

- Are you able to rest when life slows down and patiently wait for opportunities? Or are you restless and fantasizing about imaginary futures?

- Are you utilizing secrecy to strengthen your work, or do you always talk about your plans and find that you frequently don't follow through or that you are swayed by others' opinions?

- Are you swiftly seizing opportunities as soon as they arise? Or are you hesitating and letting them slip away?

- Are you enduring your setbacks with strength and grace, or are you indulging in self-pity at the first sign of difficulty?

- Are you surrendering to the flow of life, or are you resisting it while demanding it be different?

When you act like a hunter, you have the power to move through any challenge. You'll be able to act when the time is right, and rest otherwise. You'll have a method of dealing with your feelings when things don't go your way.

Practice: Gazing

To endure the trials of the hunt, we need strong determination and unbending intent. If our intent is flimsy, we won't last long. Only with unbending intent do we stand a chance at overcoming our obstacles.

In this practice, you'll gaze at a single point, such as a candle flame, a dot on the wall, or even the moon. Set a timer for three to five minutes. Sit comfortably, take a few deep breaths, and relax. Make sure your focal point is located where you can comfortably look at it.

Rest your open eyes on the object. For the duration of the session, your goal is to keep your eyes locked on it with unbending intent. Your eyes may become restless and wander away; bring them back to the object as soon as you can. Unlike the other meditation exercises that should be done gently, this gazing exercise should be done with intense focus.

When the timer rings, close your eyes. Dwell in the darkness for a moment. Savor the way your whole system feels now. Maybe you're drained and exhausted. Good. That means you stretched a new muscle. Eventually, you'll find this practice brings you clarity and energy.

When you find this practice has become easy, try extending the time between blinks. Set an intention to not blink for the duration of the exercise and see what happens. Soften your gaze and see if there is an ease in slowing down this automatic response.

By focusing all your energy on a single point, you're sharpening your unbending intent. Once you have enough self-mastery to keep your eyes open for longer periods of time, you'll be a formidable force who won't be easily deterred.

The more you practice gazing, the more you'll find your ability to focus in daily life increasing exponentially. Try practicing this exercise before a test, an important interview, or a stressful confrontation. Rather than cramming, planning, or preparing obsessively, focus all your energy and attention to the present moment by gazing. Then, you'll be fully ready to engage the situation with clarity and concentration.

Moving Forward

Through learning to hunt, Jane opened her own healing practice that combined her nursing skills and alternative modalities. Immersing herself in the spiritual community, she forged new friendships and discovered a sense of belonging.

As she disengaged from her unsupportive family and stood up for her boundaries, her family softened up eventually and curbed their hurtful behavior. They gradually settled into a more peaceful relationship. As she established a fulfilling career doing what she wanted, her family even came to respect her for following her own path, even if they didn't understand it.

Buoyed by the satisfaction of having successfully shifted her career and family dynamic, Jane was vibrant with positive energy that attracted amazing people to her. When she shifted her focus to hunting love, she applied the same strategy to gradually develop a partnership without sabotaging it with insecurity and overthinking.

When we first met, Jane was timid, joyless, and defeated. But within just a few years of practicing the Way of the Hunter, she had transformed herself and initiated a massive career change, realigned the dynamic in her family, and found the friendship, love, and community she'd been craving. She still faces many challenges, but now she knows how to meet them like a hunter.

The Gardener and the Hunter Working Together

The ways of hunting and gardening are two sides of the same coin. Utilize both simultaneously to fully realize your vision. Grow your garden joyfully and hunt your prey with cool resolve. Don't try to create your projects as a hunter, since creation should be joyful and fulfilling. Don't try to solve your problems as a gardener, or you will cave under the pressure.

Whether you're writing a book or a business plan, be a gardener while working on writing it and a hunter when selling it. For love, cultivate the garden of your social life to draw in your mate, but be a hunter when you've determined that this is your partner and you want to commit to them. In a drawn-out legal battle, rest in your garden when there's nothing to be done and become a hunter when it's time to advocate for yourself.

Of course, you can't possibly walk these ways if your body, heart, mind, and spirit are out of balance, which is why we start with that work first. Without that balance, you'll create the wrong fruit and hunt the wrong prey. And you can't use your power purposefully unless you have inner peace and presence.

All these teachings and their corresponding practices are mutually supportive. By being and not-doing, and then balancing your physical, emotional, mental, and spiritual energies, you'll have maximum power to create your dreams and capture your desires. When acting in this manner, you'll finally walk a path with heart, or a life bursting with meaning.

Now you understand the value of peace, presence, power, and purpose. You know how to balance your body, heart, mind, and spirit. You know the Way of the Gardener and the Way of the Hunter, and you know how these strategies are deployed to create your dreams and capture your desires. We'll conclude our journey with one final look at the character of the happy warrior and what it really means to walk the path of inner peace and outer power.

Chapter Eight

Walking the Path

Back when I was working in a job I hated and drowning in my depression of not achieving my artistic goals, it's no surprise that my attendance started to slip at work. Finally, I'd racked up so many points for being late and missing shifts that I was just one point away from being fired. The last time my manager spoke with me about it, he was very clear: if I was going to be late again, I shouldn't bother coming in at all.

With the job on the other side of town, the rush hour commute was at least an hour, so of course the day came when I got off to a late start (as had happened many times before) and I was desperately nudging through bumper-to-bumper traffic praying that I'd make it to work on time. I wove around cars, ran red lights, and cut off anyone in my way to buy myself every spare second. My whole life depended on this job, and I had no safety net. I simply couldn't afford to lose it.

But when I pulled into the parking lot, I was still twelve minutes late—one minute past the eleven-minute grace period. That was it. I knew I'd be fired. The familiar feeling of failure washed over me. Going in and working my shift would have been the responsible thing to do, but my spirit told me not to bother. Besides, I was in no condition to go in now with my eyes red and puffy. But it was still rush hour and I wasn't about to sit in another hour of traffic to get home.

So instead of going into work or driving home, I got out of my car and just wandered the neighborhood. I'd never spent time there except to work, so I meandered the avenues, admiring the houses and trees. I'd gotten into the habit by then of taking occasional spirit walks where I would wander and let natural signs like the direction of the wind or flying birds dictate which way I would go, so that day I followed a murder of crows, weaving haphazardly through residential streets, until I suddenly found myself on a familiar block. I knew I'd been here before, but when?

Then I noticed a woman sitting on the front porch of a nearby building. As I walked closer, I realized that I recognized her—she was a friend of mine. And as I got even closer, I could see my friend was crying. She was surprised to see me—it must have been as though I appeared out of nowhere. I asked her what was wrong, and she told me that she'd just found out that she had cancer.

All my preoccupation and self-pity about my job instantly vanished, and I spent the rest of the day with her. I had followed my intuition to a friend in need and was able to be there for her at a crucial moment. Later, when I had the chance to reflect, I was astounded to realize that even when I felt that my path was going nowhere, I was still living my purpose whether I knew it or not. I was still scared to lose my job, but I decided to trust that spirit didn't lead me to help my friend at my expense. Something else was in store for me.

The next day, I drove back to work, bracing myself for the inevitable. But when I entered the store, my manager didn't pull me aside to send me home. No one said anything at all. Curious, I logged in to the system to see how many points I had accumulated. I expected to see the dreaded third point for tardiness, but I was surprised to see only two points. Dumbfounded, I then noticed that not only did I not get a point for being late, but the system showed that I had punched in and out the day before and worked a full shift. I got paid for the day I didn't show up.

Charting Your Course

No matter which path you choose to follow, the truth is that you always end up where you started: with yourself. You may work hard to develop yourself inside and out, but no matter how far you go, or how successful you become, or how many friends or lovers you have, you'll one day move on, just as those before us have. None of it lasts. And that's okay; we're making room for those who come after us, and hopefully brightening the path just a little for others on the way. You'll solve countless challenges in your life only to graduate to the next one, but with experience and insight you'll be equipped to handle them with confidence.

If you walk one path simply in order to reach the destination, you'll be disappointed to find there is no destination. The only real way to move through life is to choose a path with meaning, a path with heart. The path of the happy warrior is one such path, though there are others. What matters is that you choose one that has meaning for you.

Choosing consciously to walk the path of the happy warrior is not a single decision, but a choice that's made repeatedly, day by day, minute by minute. Paths are always opening before you, so it's your responsibility to determine which is the best one for you. When you choose one with meaning and heart, you can easily walk it with joy.

While the Ways of the Gardener and Hunter are strategies for creating and capturing, walking the path of the happy warrior is more of a general attitude for living. When you must decide what to study in college, or what career to pursue, or where to live, you can't rely only on logic or emotion. Curiosity will lead you to discover which of the options available to you has the most meaning.

It may be logical to chase money. It may be emotionally satisfying to chase fantasies. But curiosity will offer a path that's fulfilling right from the first step because the exploration itself is the source of excitement. While you still pursue goals, you don't wait for success to be joyful. You find joy in the privilege of getting to do what you're doing.

At its core, walking your path means never betraying your spirit. It means honoring your values and valuing your curiosity. If your spirit is curious about a direction that seems unrealistic, give it some consideration and discover where it might lead. That does not mean you should be irresponsible, reckless, or impractical. It means you should make decisions from your highest spirit self, and then apply the ways of hunting and gardening to accomplish your doings practically, responsibly, and effectively.

Walking a path is also about prioritizing the ultimate value of harmony above all else. It means remaining openhearted and deeply connected to people around you. Choosing a path of meaning and heart means being compassionate and empathetic toward others while still maintaining your boundaries and not giving your power away. It means that you should seek solutions that benefit the whole, and not just yourself. When you act in this way, you'll find that your own needs and desires become naturally fulfilled. If you prioritize harmony for all, you too will enjoy the sweetness of that harmony.

Shapeshifting

Sometimes, the path we choose may lose its meaning or become stagnant or untenable, and it becomes necessary to stop, reassess, and choose a different way. This can be challenging, because we often cling to what we know; we don't want to betray our previous choices or "waste" previous effort. But if the path you're on has lost its heart, it doesn't make sense to stay on it. If your curiosity has shifted in a new direction, have the courage to follow it. You may dedicate yourself to a path for decades and drop it in a heartbeat when your spirit commands. And that makes sense; we aren't just one thing for the duration of our lives—we evolve and have many roles and interests over time. It's not about choosing a path and rigidly sticking to it no matter what. It's about tuning in to your own curiosity and letting it have the final say over your desires, feelings, and thoughts.

When you're willing and able to drop and change paths as needed, you become a shapeshifter. Shapeshifting also encompasses the power to adopt any role as the situation demands, without clinging to one identity for all circumstances. Sometimes you should assert strength and power, while other times adopting gentleness and passivity might better suit you. By shifting roles on command, you can become whatever the moment needs.

Consider Jackie Chan in his role as the mischievous Drunken Master: a master martial artist who masks his power under the guise of being a drunken buffoon. The

Drunken Master is at peace with himself, he is present, and so he is powerful. But since he walks a path consciously chosen, a path with heart and meaning, he doesn't need others to fear or respect him to know that he's formidable. Only the weak insist on displaying their power at every turn, while the strong are content to let others think they're weak because they know they're not. The wise shapeshifting trickster uses her opponents' underestimation of her as a shield and a weapon to outwit them.

If you're too proud to humble yourself, you're not walking a path—you're clinging to a stale identity. Let your opponents underestimate you at their own peril.

Accept All Outcomes

Ultimately, as you make your way along your chosen path, you'll experience setbacks, losses, and defeats. We can imagine our positive vision and set things in motion and all can be going well, but life inevitably has a way of throwing challenges into the mix. So how do we utilize positive thinking effectively when disappointment and defeat are looming?

By accepting all outcomes. Whenever you pursue something, you're taking a risk that you won't get it. Obviously, you want success and fear failure. But what if the worst possible outcome that you could imagine might turn out to be amazing in ways you can't yet understand? When you accept all outcomes as potentially being for the good, you can never be disappointed, only pleasantly surprised.

If you're single-mindedly pursuing a goal, accept that you may not reach it, and imagine how that may be because there are even more exciting paths you would never have considered otherwise. If you want to find a permanent life partner, accept that you may not, and imagine how you might be even fuller on your own. If you want to have a baby, accept that you may not, and imagine how fostering, adopting, raising animals, or simply living for yourself may be even more meaningful.

Accepting all outcomes—even the most unimaginably horrific ones—is true power. When you accept all outcomes, you can't be disappointed. You don't become attached to things being a certain way. You come to trust in your own power to keep going and thriving, rather than depending on a happy ending to keep you satisfied.

There is no finish line. Having solved a challenge, you'll be faced with a heavier one. There is no end to the path. So enjoy the moment happening right now, the life unfolding in front of your face each day. Don't rest your hopes on an uncertain future; anchor in your own power to field whatever this mysterious life throws at you and to build whatever your curiosity guides you to on this path.

Afterword

The Final Secret

Fulfilling your purpose in life is not about uncovering some preordained destiny. Rather, it is the practice of fully accessing the present moment, harnessing inner peace, bringing outer power to bear, and then manifesting what you will. Spirit did not predetermine your fate in a polished manuscript. Spirit manifests as you, which means your choices are what determine your path, and not the mystical force of fate. That means you are the point where fate meets free will.

Fate and destiny are simply the aspects of your experiences you can't control: the moment you were born and the moment you will die, and all the weather every day in between. Fate does not determine the course you take between your birth and your death, however, any more than it determines how you respond to the weather on any given day, because that's up to you. We're all manifesting our lives, but we mostly do it unintentionally. Inner peace and outer power are about creating a container in which you can manifest a life of meaning with unbending intent.

To properly utilize your personal power, first you practice being and not-doing to cultivate inner peace and presence. In that state, you're able to engage the present moment and participate fully. With inner peace comes outer power.

While cultivating peace, presence, and power through not-doing, you also need to properly balance peace and power within your body, heart, mind, and spirit to make your doings effective.

Don't indulge all your body's desires, but rather use the body to accumulate power and good health. The body is a temple to your spirit and should be revered as such. Your physical power should then be used to nurture, protect, and defend, rather than dominate others. Don't let the body's cravings determine your life choices.

Don't indulge all your heart's feelings, but rather use the heart to connect with others by sharing your feelings and letting them go. Be openhearted and ready to give away your attachments to have a full heart. Don't hide, suppress, or lie about your feelings, but experience them fully, share them, and then let them go. Don't let the heart's longings determine your life choices.

Don't indulge all your mind's thoughts, but rather use the mind to acquire knowledge. Be open-minded and absorb knowledge from a wide variety of sources. Let your worldview be flexible and open to change. Train your mind to rest so you can better hear your spiritual curiosity. Don't let the mind's fear decide your life choices.

But do indulge your spirit's childlike curiosity. Let the spirit decide your life choices. Remember that desires have definite objects, feelings have definite expectations, and thoughts have definite assumptions about reality. But curiosity is open-ended, it poses a question without giving you an answer. If you engage that question, you'll be amazed at where the thread of curiosity leads you.

When your four powers are in harmony, you're ready to act with power and purpose. To cultivate prosperity, abundance, and satisfaction, follow the Way of the Gardener.

Plant all your creative seeds without judging them. Nurture all your creative seeds joyfully, allowing your curiosity to flit from seed to seed. When a particular plant sprouts faster than the others, then you'll know to focus on that one exclusively. Do not mistake the fruit for the reward. The fruit is only the fuel that sustains another cycle of working in your garden, and *that* is the reward. Don't look to the fruit of your labor to give you joy. Find joy in your labor and your work will be play.

Playing in your garden will make it grow fast and strong, whereas agitating about selling your fruit is like yelling at your seeds to grow faster. Doing so will only hurt your growth. As a gardener, you commit to building your projects brick by brick, letter by letter, one step at a time. You find joy in selecting and placing the bricks, rather than waiting to finish the building. When we practice the Way of the Gardener, we learn to get out of our own way and stop sabotaging our creativity.

For the intentions you catch rather than create, follow the Way of the Hunter. The hunter relies on five skills to catch her prey: stillness, secrecy, swiftness, strength, and surrender.

Stillness means active patience: contentedly resting as you keenly observe the world for opportunity. Secrecy means shrouding your intent so that other people's judgments do not cloud your clarity or confidence. Swiftness means seizing opportunity the moment it arises without any hesitation or deliberation. Strength means enduring the fight and refusing to wallow in self-pity in the face of defeat. Surrender means humbly accepting all outcomes, allowing the flow of life to carry you without resistance. After surrender, you return to stillness, again resting and watching for the next opportunity.

In this manner, you can maintain your focus and stamina for the long haul without becoming exhausted. As a hunter, you will be patient, confident, fearless, driven, and grounded. You'll be a warrior ready to take on the battle of your life. But you won't just be a warrior—you'll be a *happy* warrior.

The Life of the Happy Warrior

The happy warrior has a serious purpose and deeply held values, but they don't take the game of life too seriously. They don't expect to win their fight, but they fight because it's the right thing to do in the moment. They act because they know it's correct, regardless of the outcome.

A happy warrior is impervious to insults and personal attacks. They know that bad behavior from others only reveals the character of the attacker, and not them. A happy warrior cannot be defeated, because even in the face of seeming defeat, they are content to have done their best. They find joy in simply exercising their power for a good, worthwhile purpose. If the path has meaning and heart, then it doesn't matter if they reach the end goal or not—they are fulfilled by walking the path itself.

Only when you engage life's conflicts as a happy warrior will you have the joyful power to see you through difficulties. With the foundation of inner peace that allows you to be present, the alignment of your body, heart, mind, and spirit, the ways of gardening and hunting, walking your path, shapeshifting through roles, accepting all outcomes, and living as a happy warrior, you'll enjoy a life bursting with meaning.

The Great Secret

So as you may have figured out already, the Great Secret is secret not in the sense that it's hidden from the uninitiated. It's secret only in the sense that it is hard to see because it's so simple. It's secret because it's an obvious truth that's difficult to grasp and live by. It's secret because you can't predict the magical places the path will take you, because every aspect of this path is performed internally with how you relate to your thoughts, feelings, and senses. No one can see the mindset with which you approach your life, but they'll all see your fullness and sense your power.

Now the secret is yours to keep, practice, and share. These teachings are cumulative; the more you practice, the stronger your skills will get. Don't be discouraged if you find it difficult at first, just keep applying the teachings to your own development. Enjoy the process of practicing and seeing growth rather than waiting for the joy of accomplishment.

When you practice and strengthen these essential skills, you'll be bursting with power and positivity. You'll expect setbacks, so you won't be disappointed by them. You'll be prepared to handle whatever life throws at you. You'll be peaceful amid sorrow, composed amid chaos, dignified in defeat, and gracious in victory.

True power is not about knowing everything all the time or perfectly accomplishing everything. Power is the ability to be here and now and to bring all your energy under the focus of your will and to trust that you only need to know what you need to know when you need to know it, and not a moment sooner. You can't know or understand everything all the time. Having power doesn't mean deluding yourself into thinking you're in control of everything in your life. Having power means knowing that you have little control but embracing uncertainty anyway.

A person with power walks their path one step at a time without ever looking too far ahead or too far behind. They confidently drive into the darkness without knowing where the road will lead. They drive ahead not with fear, but with curiosity. Their curiosity to see where the road might lead is what delights them. They're not waiting to get home but just enjoying the drive.

So stop waiting for your destiny to find you! Stop searching for your life purpose! Stop wondering what you're meant to do!

Instead, choose your own adventure by listening to your spirit's curiosity. Cultivate your purpose by gardening your seeds and hunting your prey. Align your powers so that you naturally fulfill your purpose in each moment, whether you realize it or not. Trust that your purpose is being fulfilled even in your darkest hour, even when you can't see how.

You may never fully appreciate the purpose that you've fulfilled, because you can't witness all the ways you've touched other people's lives. But if you walk your path, if you seek harmony, if you are present in each moment, then you will profoundly change people's lives and the world just by being who you are. All you must do is return to the present moment and remember that with inner peace comes outer power.

Acknowledgments

Our accomplishments are not our own but belong to everyone who helped us along the way.

First and foremost, I must offer deep and eternal gratitude to Randy Davila. Thank you for believing in me and encouraging me to write this book. Your guidance and support have been an enormous blessing.

Special thanks to Sara Sutterfield Winn whose notes were instrumental in guiding me. Thanks to everyone at Hierophant Publishing for all their hard work providing the world so many powerful spiritual teachings.

Thank you to my incredible wife Katelyn for supporting me through all the hard days and being the true model of a happy warrior. You are the greatest teacher I've ever had.

Thank you to my sister Pritam for always being there for me no matter what. Endless thanks to my parents Yesmin and Salim for all their hard work and sacrifice.

My deepest gratitude to the many teachers, guides, and mentors who shared their wisdom with me and helped me find my way when I was lost.

Finally, thanks to all the people I've had the pleasure of working with through my healing practice. I am humbled and honored to play my small part in each of your spiritual journeys.

About the Author

Shaman Nabeel Redwood is a shamanic healer, spiritual teacher, and personal coach based in Los Angeles. As the founder of Shamanic Healing LA, he has served thousands of clients and grown a vibrant community of seekers all over the world. Visit him at shamanichealingla.com.

Hierophant publishing

books that inspire your body, mind, and spirit

San Antonio, TX
www.hierophantpublishing.com